INDEPENDENCE TOWNSHIP LIBRARY

3 4633 00231 1668

Head of Household

Head of Household

Money Management for Single Parents

Kara Stefan

PRAEGER

An Imprint of ABC-CLIO, LLC

A B C ⬥ C L I O

Santa Barbara, California • Denver, Colorado • Oxford, England

Copyright © 2009 by Kara Stefan

All rights reserved. No part of this publication may be reproduced, stored in a retrieval system, or transmitted, in any form or by any means, electronic, mechanical, photocopying, recording, or otherwise, except for the inclusion of brief quotations in a review, without prior permission in writing from the publisher.

Library of Congress Cataloging-in-Publication Data

Stefan, Kara.
    Head of household : money management for single parents / Kara Stefan.
        p. cm.
    Includes bibliographical references and index.
    ISBN 978-0-313-36284-2 (hard copy : alk. paper) — ISBN 978-0-313-36285-9 (ebook)
1. Single parents—Finance, Personal. 2. Values. 3. Parenting. I. Title.
HG179.S817   2009
332.0240085—dc22   2009012868

13 12 11 10 9   1 2 3 4 5

This book is also available on the World Wide Web as an eBook.
Visit www.abc-clio.com for details.

ABC-CLIO, LLC
130 Cremona Drive, P.O. Box 1911
Santa Barbara, California 93116-1911

This book is printed on acid-free paper ∞

Manufactured in the United States of America

3 4633 00231 1668

For my boys, always in my heart;
and Indigo, always at my feet.

Contents

List of Tables and Figure

ONE

Introduction

This book is about values as much as anything. You'll read about what constitutes good value, especially in consideration of the particular challenges and advantages of single parenting.

For single parents in particular, lifestyle shouldn't just be about good value for the money we pay for goods and services. That's a primary guiding rule, and you'll read all about it here. But this book is about values—yours and your children's. As the head of your household, you can have the greatest influence on what your child values most, in childhood and as he or she grows into adulthood.

Do you want your child to value expensive cars and houses? Is that to be his or her driving passion and ambition in life?

Or would you like to teach them about honesty, fairness, kindness, and tolerance? Because none of these things actually cost any money. You make these little decisions every day regarding what you value. And it will leave a lasting impression on your children.

When you buy an expensive pair of shoes or piece of clothing that you could easily replace with something similar (or something you already own) for much less, you're communicating to your children that you value clothes. It's something on which you're willing to spend perhaps a disproportionate amount of the money you earn.

They may not say it, but next summer when you tell them you can't afford to send them to a summer camp, they perceive that you value clothes over their summer camp experience. In their minds, they don't see the difference between a $150 pair of shoes and an $800 camp.

It's not something you can reason out with them. In fact, you may choose not to reason it out for yourself because it's an uncomfortable prospect.

A lot of single parents don't have excess discretionary income. They pay for the things that they have to pay for, and what little is left over they often make small splurges for the family, maybe occasionally take them out to eat or bowling. It's tough to know when you should save that money and what small difference it might make, as opposed to the instant reward and gratification of making you and/or your children happy.

Your decisions in those situations are what drive your values, and that's what your children see, and learn, and eventually imitate.

ENJOY WHAT'S GOOD

For most single parents, it's not practical to have a lot of materialistic "wants." We already have a whole lot of really necessary "needs." So value is about adjusting your mind-set to appreciate what you have.

If you and your children are in good health, that's the most valuable asset you can have.

If you have a job you like or work you enjoy doing (even if you don't like your employer), you are already head and shoulders above most people, even those who make a whole lot of money.

The same applies to single parenting. It's a lifestyle, whether you choose it or not. And with the right mind-set, it can be an incredibly enjoyable lifestyle.

I recently read that single moms tend to suffer less stress at the end of the workday than other working moms because they don't have to come home to the expectation, to whatever degree, that they need to have dinner on the table by a certain time.

Single parents, being the sole grown-up in the household, get to set the dinner time. And it can vary every night. If you don't feel like cooking meat loaf and homemade mashed potatoes for dinner, or even canned ravioli, you can serve ice cream with a side of carrots if you like. Ice cream is healthy. There's no one there to judge you or tell you otherwise. Except for your children, and they'll think you're terrific.

Divorce Can Broaden a Child's Horizons

When my parents divorced back in the 1970s, my dad moved into a small apartment in downtown Savannah. That was cool, because we lived primarily in our family home with my mom in the suburbs, and downtown was actually far more beautiful and full of things to do. My dad, brother, and I would wander among the grassy squares and into old bookstores, anti-que shops, diners, and check out the waterfront. We would go to baseball games, bowling, and putt-putt, then out for pizza and ice cream. We did these things far more often than we ever did when he lived at home.

It was a far cry from our two-story house with a chain-link fence on the south side of town. Every other weekend, we got the best of both worlds. City and suburbs. Such is the life when two married people became single parents. My brother and I were none the worse for it. In fact, we broad-ened our horizons, learned how to be flexible, and discovered our parents weren't perfect.

It kind of takes the burden off parenting when your kids finally realize that.

SINGLE VERSUS MARITAL "BLISS"

What a person feels when learning he or she is going to become a single parent really isn't too far off what a married parent feels. That is, generally fear and apprehension. But what many single parents forget to feel is the pure joy. You can get so weighed down by financial worries, child care concerns, family pressure and judgments, and your own self-doubt: "How will I be able to do this alone? Will anyone ever love me with a child in tow?"

Sure, the burdens are heavy. But burdens of marriage are heavy as well. Look at the issues that you don't have to concern yourself when you're a single parent:

- Culinary skills to produce a varied repertoire of dinner meals;
- Respectable laundry and housekeeping skills;
- Sharing your embarrassing bad habits, such as flossing in the shower and then sticking it to the tile wall and forgetting about it;
- Worse yet, enduring your spouse's bad habits;
- Combining furniture, like his wine barrel poker table;
- Discussions, let alone arguments, about how to spend your money;
- Joint debt;
- In-laws;
- Not always going on the vacation of your choice;
- Feeling the pressure to meet someone else's expectations, or help them meet theirs;

- The toilet seat dilemma (up or down?);
- Committing to one, non-blood-related person for the rest of your life;
- Are you really in love? Is this really the one? What is love, anyway?;
- Conditional love.

These are not generally concerns of a single parent. Here's why:

- Children often prefer to eat the same thing every night;
- Children don't care if their clothes are wrinkled or even dirty for that matter (until they become teenagers, and by then they can launder their clothes themselves);
- Children don't even notice your bad habits;
- You can shape their habits, before they become bad;
- You get to pick out all the furniture;
- You get to decide how your money is spent;
- Your debt is yours alone;
- No in-laws;
- You get to choose and plan all of your vacations;
- You only have to deal with your own expectations;
- Your toilet seat preference—children are trainable;
- You may date whom you like;
- You may ponder questions of love for as long as you like, with no wedding deadlines;
- Your children will love you unconditionally. All your life, they may be the only ones who will.

THE PRIVILEGE OF PARENTING

What's important to remember is that becoming a parent is a privilege. An honor. It is the single most important thing you will ever do with your life. Even presidents, CEOs of major corporations, and rulers of countries—anyone you can think of that has an important position or has achieved a major accomplishment—cannot escape this awesome responsibility. If you are a bad parent, then no matter how successful you are elsewhere in your life, you are still a bad parent.

And guess what. Being married is not a prerequisite for being a good parent.

I have always believed that you really have to work at becoming a bad parent. Children emerge from the womb as innocent beings. Most of the time parenting is just a matter of lending guidance and not screwing up in some way.

ADJUST YOUR MIND

Single parents have it good in a lot of ways. Notwithstanding having to pay child support or alimony, for the most part your money is yours. It may not be much, but it's yours. No one is sharing or monitoring your bank account. So if you want to buy something for yourself, you can.

You can choose where to go for your vacation. No compromises. You can choose the couch you want for the living room. I once heard of a couple in which the husband wanted a blue couch and the wife wanted a maroon couch so they compromised and bought a green couch. No one got what they wanted.

The grass may look greener in another yard; but there are always weeds to pull no matter how pristine that lawn may appear.

When you're a single parent, you can buy what you want. You can choose whether or not to let your children have a say in those types of decisions. You can even pick and choose which decisions in which they can and can't have a say.

However, single parents often have to rely on a single income. Even factoring in child support or alimony payments, life is typically a bit leaner when single with children than when married with children. So you can choose the couch you want, but only within the price range you can afford.

When you think about it though, that is also true for married folks. Everyone has a price range; single parents perhaps a little lower. That's the trade-off for the ability to buy a red couch if you want a red couch. Not a bad trade for a little independence once in awhile.

The single parent lifestyle can be extremely enjoyable and rewarding. One of the best rewards in life is accomplishing something on your own, and there's really no accomplishment greater in life than raising children. Ergo, a single parent can receive the highest reward: Doing one of the greatest things in life, and accomplishing it on your own.

You just have to adjust your mind to see it that way.

DOLLARS AND SENSE

Because many people become single parents due to unfortunate circumstances, it's not always viewed as a wonderful lifestyle. However, more and more adults are choosing to face this unique challenge with a positive and empowered outlook.

The primary setback for most single parents is money. Therefore, perhaps more than anyone else, single parents need a financial education. For a single parent in particular, it's easy to become overwhelmed, focus only on what's in front of you, and ignore the type of financial education and planning that can make single parenting easier and more rewarding.

This guide will provide must-know information as it relates specifically to single-parenting financial challenges. Paying for family housing, health care, and child care can be an enormous burden on a single salary. And at the crux of it all, most single parents are trying to raise their children to a standard similar to what their friends enjoy—so it's helpful to learn how to stretch your salary, know where to cut corners, and when not to.

There are also some remarkably positive financial aspects to single parenting, such as the head of household tax filing status, single parent rates for places such as gym membership, and teens of single parents applying for college scholarships and financial aid.

You don't have to make a lot of money to be a financially successful single parent. No matter how much you earn, it's important to know how to manage it. Armed with easily digestible financial guidance, single parents can take control of their financial matters and learn to enjoy all the perks and rewards of the single parent lifestyle.

NO SHORTCUTS

What you won't find in this book is a quick and easy get-rich scheme. Consider earning money as similar to raising children—why do it in a hurry? Each stage of a child's life is so interesting and entertaining (even those awful teenage years), you wouldn't dream of skipping over any part just to get to the end destination.

Raising children is a journey, and so is earning money. It often takes longer to do and acquire the "things" you want when you're single as opposed to being married, when there's typically either two salaries or one salary plus child and home care. Perhaps it takes a few more years to buy your first house. You may run a little behind on saving and investing. You probably won't be the first in line for the latest high-tech gadget or newest model car each year.

That's not such a bad thing though. The longer you wait and work for the things you acquire, the more they'll mean to you. They have more value to you, and that's the sort of value you want to teach your children.

If you raise children from scratch (literally) as a single parent, they may grow up knowing not to ask for too much. If you've had to downsize your lifestyle as a newly single parent due to widowhood or divorce, then it's going to take awhile for your children to learn to adjust to a lower standard of living. For you as well. But soon your children will learn to "pick their battles," and only ask for things they truly value. Don't feel badly that you can't buy them everything they want. No one should get every thing they want because they don't learn to value what they receive.

High-net parents will tell you, they have the devil of a time teaching these all-important values to their "entitled" children. As a single parent, you've got it easy. Saying "no" to expensive or superfluous purchases becomes inherent in your lifestyle. It's a necessity.

One of the rewards of single parenting is that it's easier to teach the value of money to your children. If you embrace this reality instead of resent it, your financial education—and your peace of mind—will come more easily.

TWO

Budget

As single parents, our instinct is often to overcompensate. For whatever reason, our children are not engaged daily with two parents, and we feel bad about that. So we go out to dinner, plan expensive activities, and hold extravagant birthday parties. Stop.

Realize that your child's basic human desires are not affected by your soul-mate status. He will always want pizza for dinner. She will always want a princess birthday party. It's up to you—single or not—to set appropriate limits.

And remember that your child's most basic human desire is to procure your time, your undivided attention, your laughter and unfettered happiness as opposed to being stressed out by finances. If holding a cookie-decorating birthday party in your home is cheaper and less stressful than two overstimulating hours at Chuck E. Cheese, do it. Your son or daughter will be wired either way.

Do what allows you to experience less stress. Use some of the money you save to hire a teenager to help you run the party if it will help ease your burden and allow you to enjoy the party.

Remember that, particularly for a single parent, your time is more important than your money. It's easy to forget this. Don't waste your time doing things that are not worth the savings reward.

For example, clipping coupons. Unless you really enjoy this and get your children involved, don't waste your Sunday sitting around clipping coupons. It could take an hour or more and in the end just save you a few bucks. If you save at all. You may also fall prey to clipping coupons for stuff you wouldn't have bought otherwise. Not to mention that coupons are typically offered for unhealthy, prepackaged goods. When was the last time you clipped a coupon for a bag of apples?

Your time as a single parent is worth way more than a few coupons can offer—to you and to your children. A better strategy is to check to see if the manufacturer has a mailing list for which you can sign up for the things that you buy on a regular basis. Many times manufacturers send their best coupons, samples, and rebates to the people on their mailing lists. This is especially true for manufacturers of diapers, formula, baby food, cleaning supplies, and personal care products. In other words, target your high-expense items and let the manufacturers do the work of getting the exact coupons you need directly to you.

Really think about how you spend your time, and whether it's truly good for your family. Spend Sundays outdoors with your children.

THE EGREGIOUS "BUDGET"

At the very thought of crafting and following a budget, your first thought may be, "ugh." However, a budget can be one of the most creative and effective tools in your financial war chest.

Your budget is what allows you to have discretionary income at the end of the month. Follow it, and that new car, sofa, or <insert-here-whatever-you-want> may be yours after a set period of time.

A budget can help make decision-making easier—should I buy this or that? You buy what's in your budget, and pay the amount for which it was budgeted. Simple.

It's also a great value to pass on to your children. "Can I get an <insert-here>? Why not?"

"It's not in our budget."

It can become your go-to excuse for everything, with the added prestige of appearing to be in complete control of your financial matters.

Finally, an acceptable substitute for "Because I said so."

THE LESS YOU HAVE, THE EASIER TO BUDGET

The less you earn, the less you can buy. And therefore, the less you have to clean, maintain, fix, insure, nourish, or spend time on. Yay.

The less you earn, the simpler your life can be. This includes establishing a budget. Create an incoming column for all of your income sources (salary, commissions/bonuses, child support, alimony, benefit checks, etc.). Then draft an outgoing column for all of your expenses (see Table A).

Table A   Sample Budget I

	Actual spending vs. budget	
	Actual ($)	Budgeted ($)
Income	3,500.00	3,500.00
Expenses	3,395.00	3,450.00
Remainder	**105.00**	**50.00**

If your life is simple, so are your expenses. It's easy to determine what is necessary in order to maintain your household, like food, utilities, transportation, child care, and housing expenses. Among these are fixed and variable expenses. For example, your rent or mortgage may be the same every month, but your utility costs may change with the seasons (see Table B).

Table B   Sample Budget II

Categories	Actual ($)	Budgeted ($)	Difference ($)
Automobile	200.00	200.00	0.00
Cash withdrawal	375.00	400.00	25.00
Children/toys	56.00	50.00	(6.00)
Clothing	62.00	75.00	13.00
Dining out	38.00	40.00	2.00
Education	30.00	50.00	20.00
Entertainment	85.00	40.00	(45.00)
Fees	45.00	55.00	10.00
Gifts	12.00	10.00	(2.00)
Groceries	407.00	400.00	(7.00)
Health care	150.00	150.00	0.00
Hobbies/leisure	25.00	25.00	0.00
Household	105.00	100.00	(5.00)
Insurance	125.00	125.00	0.00
Miscellaneous	40.00	50.00	10.00
Mortgage/rent	1,200.00	1,200.00	0.00
Personal care	35.00	50.00	15.00
Pet care	0.00	20.00	20.00
Phone/wireless	58.00	60.00	2.00
Utilities	347.00	350.00	3.00
Total expenses	**3,395.00**	**3,450.00**	**55.00**

Then there are discretionary expenses, like dining out, swim lessons, and a new pair of shoes.

Often it may feel as if there is a fine line between necessary and discretionary expenses, but consider that your values sit precariously along that line. For example, for some people things like a cell phone and cable television may be necessities. For others, those are expendable expenditures they can do without. Many people can afford them but choose not to so that they can have extra money for vacations or pay for extracurricular activities for their children, like soccer or swimming.

The difference between necessary and discretionary is a very personal decision that reflects your values—you are likely to spend money on the things that are important to you.

Once you establish your budget and determine what you value as necessary versus discretionary, plug in estimates of how much each item costs. Your budget may change seasonally based on changes in utility prices, etc. You can look up old bills or checkbook stubs or your online payment history to get ballpark and/or exact costs for each expense in your budget.

There are dozens of online and software programs out there you can use to develop a household budget, including Quicken and Microsoft. But don't go buy anything until you check out what's already on your own computer. You're likely to find something there that was included in your software bundle, like the Microsoft Office Suite. Even the standard Excel program offers a template for a family monthly budget planner, and more free templates are available to download at the Microsoft Web site, as well as other Web sites.

You can spend money to develop a budget, but if you have a computer, chances are good you've already got something you can adapt for your use. And even if you don't, nothing beats pen and paper for hands-on records management.

PAY YOURSELF FIRST

Hopefully, once you pay off your necessary expenses, each month you'll have money left over to pay for discretionary expenses—which may also change seasonally. However, first determine an amount that should be allotted, on a regular basis, to your long-term goals. This is very important. No matter how little money you have or earn, it's important to save for one or more long-term goals.

This is what will make you feel good about yourself—more than a new pair of shoes or toys for your children or going out to dinner. Knowing that you have, once again, each month, set aside money to buy a house or pay for college or provide income during retirement. This really will make you feel good about yourself, so it's a very important step in your financial management.

Even if you're wallowing in debt, it's important to feel that you're working to build a net worth even as you pay off your net deficit. More importantly, you are building self-worth. And self-worth is a far more valuable asset than net worth, and a tangible value to pass on to your children.

One of the first tenets of investing for the future is to "pay yourself first." This means that you value yourself and your long-term goals. Funding your own goals is an expense that goes under the "necessary" column of your budget. When you "pay yourself first," the first outgo from your paycheck is paid into a savings or investment account.

It is best to set up an automatic, scheduled deposit system whereby money is automatically transferred from your checking account into your long-term savings or investment account before you even miss it. Before you pay your other necessary bills. Before you even think about what to do with leftover discretionary money. Paying yourself first is a regular, necessary, long-term expense.

One of the best ways to do this is through an employer-sponsored retirement plan at work, such as a 401(k). Many employers will give you the option to transfer money from your paycheck into your 401(k) or similar plan before it even gets direct deposited to your bank.

One of the added advantages of a qualified retirement plan is that the money is deducted from your paycheck before income taxes are assessed. This means that your income is reduced, so the subsequent taxes are less. This is what it means to make tax-deductible contributions to your retirement account. It also means you pay fewer taxes throughout the year.

PAY YOUR BILLS NEXT

Next, naturally you have to pay off all of your bills. Obviously, very important but a significant point here is to ensure that you always pay your credit cards—at very least the minimum amount—on time. As discussed further in the Credit section of this book, your credit history and score are the keys to your financial success.

Other people may earn more money than you and have lots more expensive goodies, but if you have good credit, it's the finance world equivalent to good health.

DISCRETIONARY INCOME, LAST

Finally, after you've paid yourself and all your bills and valued expenses, you may decide what to do with the balance left over—also known as your "discretionary income." This means you actually have a choice of where to spend your money, and how much you allot to your choices.

Soccer, ballet, karate, swim lessons, birthday parties, Christmas gifts and decorations, vacations, pool memberships, clothes, household decor, toys, dining out—all of it. Pick and choose what you can afford, based on what you value and the values you want your children to learn.

Your choices should be personal, based on what you really want and what's best for your family. In other words, don't try to keep up with what other people have or are doing with their time and money. This can be tough, but so can you. Stop trying to keep up with the Joneses. They're great folks, but your family has character and strong values.

Sticking to a budget is like disciplining your children. Be firm, be consistent, and praise yourself for being good.

HEAD OF HOUSEHOLD TIP: DON'T WHINE

Be not whiney or judgmental of those who spend their money on gaudy, expensive, big-screen TVs. Then maybe they'll invite you to their house to watch the Super Bowl.

Creative Budgeting: It's about Values, Not Money

Be thankful you don't have to suffer the "wagon wheel coffee table" debate scene from the movie, When Harry Met Sally. *As a single parent, you get to decorate your home for yourself and your children—not a spouse, in-laws, corporate dinner parties, neighbors, peers, parents, or to impress anyone else. Make it personal.*

In our home, I've strung twine around the perimeter of my son's bedroom and hung his artwork on the walls with clothespins. It's festive, lively, and personal. The impression it makes on people who come to my house is that I care about my children. I showcase their work, their treasures. I decorate with the things we love, that we value—like shells found at the beach, driftwood, rocks, butterfly wings, and bird feathers.

I also decorate with action figures. In my bathroom there's a moose, Batman, and a robot standing on the back rim of my sink. Three soldiers garnish the sink in the downstairs bathroom. Originally, they were tub toys set there to dry after my son's bath. Later that night I chuckled to see them there when I brushed my teeth. I decided the chuckle factor was important, so I've left them there as both a functional and decorative element. Thankfully, I'm assured to smile several times a day, no matter how bad that day is going.

BONUSES AND WINDFALLS

If you budget effectively, then you can utilize discretionary income for occasional surprises and treats for your family. This is better than using a bonus or windfall of cash to treat your family. Your treats or vacations will be more rewarding if you plan and save for them methodically. A tax refund or end-of-year bonus is not the time to think about a whirlwind trip to Disneyland. Think longer term than that.

Also, don't think of a cash windfall as a lump sum. You can divide it to fund several goals. First of all, some employers allow you to add this money to your retirement account. Again, you'll get an income tax advantage if the money is transferred from your paycheck before taxes are taken out.

If you do get a cash windfall, you can always apply a half or a third to different goals. For example, invest a third in your retirement account, contribute a third to an IRA account, and maybe save the final third toward your summer vacation.

If you simply must blow the money, put a cap on the expenses—like you can only spend $100. That way you don't go on a frivolous shopping spree, and before you know it, it's all gone.

If it's a good idea to pay down some debt, do so. But at the same time, take a portion and put it in your savings or investment account. This will help you feel like you're building toward your future, not just paying down your past.

HEAD OF HOUSEHOLD CHECKLIST FOR MANAGING EXPENSES

✓ Be realistic—if you are currently spending $400 a month on groceries, you probably are not going to be able to cut that amount in half—but you may be able to save $25–50 per month with careful planning.

✓ Grocery shop with a list in hand.

✓ Don't buy anything in volume that you don't use in volume.

✓ Don't gravitate toward a "sale" rack or shelf unless you're seeking something specific that might be there.

✓ Don't buy something just because it's on sale.
✓ Don't go shopping to alleviate boredom or kill time. Go for a walk instead.
✓ Buy only things you want or need (never anything you "could use").
✓ Pay with a debit card so you don't spend more than you have.
✓ Buy used cars for the greatest value. More than 36 percent of the United States' millionaires prefer to buy used cars, according to the book *The Millionaire Next Door*. And they tend to buy American-made cars. If you buy what you can afford and feel good about what you drive, you're in pretty rich company.

THREE

Child Care

Child care is a difficult expense whether you're single or married. Married couples who require child care most likely have two incomes. This is much easier, even if that second income is pretty much regulated to pay for child care. In contrast, single parents tend to pay a significantly higher share of their household income for child care than married couples.

The tough thing about child care is that this is the most important decision you can make—to whom do you entrust your most precious treasures? And how can you possibly complain about the expense?

The cost of child care in the United States varies greatly based on where in the country a family lives, the type of care used, and the quality. According to the National Association of Child Care Resource and Referral Agencies (2007),

- The average annual cost of full-time care for an infant ranges from $3,900 (Mississippi) to $14,591 (Massachusetts).
- The average annual cost of full-time child care for a four-year-old child ranges from $3,380 (Mississippi) to $10,787 (Massachusetts).
- The average annual cost of after-school care ranges from $2,500 (South Carolina) to $8,600 (Minnesota).

Assuming your infant is cared for the full 2,080 hours worked in a year at the lowest rate in the range, that averages out to $1.87 an hour. Even the highest rate in the country works out to only $6.46 an hour—less than you'd have to pay most teenagers babysitting for a few hours on a Friday night.

It's shocking how little we, as a country, prioritize child care. We spend way more than any of those numbers for our cars, our computers, and even our clothes.

And yet, child care remains a tremendous expense in our budget—often rivaling housing and grocery expenses.

What's important to remember is that the only thing that matters here is quality. Many times a higher price is indicative of quality, but like many consumer goods and services, this is not universally true.

A TALE OF TWO BABYSITTERS

In 1988, I engaged an Italian homemaker in San Diego, California, for full-time care in her home for my son from the time he was six months old through age four and a half years. During that entire four-year stretch, I paid only $100 a week and nothing during weeks we took vacation. I could not have received better care anywhere—she raised him as if he was one of her own. He also benefited from the company and influence, I might add, of her husband and three teenage boys.

In 2002, I engaged a retired elementary school teacher in Richmond, Virginia, for full-time care in her home for my youngest son starting from age one to nearly five years old. Again, during that entire stretch, I paid only $100 a week. Again, I could not have received better care any-where—she provided daily lesson plans and had him fully prepared to enter kindergarten as a young five-year-old.

Maybe I am the luckiest mom in the world, but to strike gold twice in two different parts of the country, 14 years apart seems a bit of a stretch. I visited a lot of day care situations. Enough to know that when I found the right one, I found the right one.

For both my budget and *my peace of mind.*

What's important to know is that many high-quality child care providers will charge only a nominal fee to supplement their household income. These are the ones you want to find; they're providing child care because they want to—it's not a business for them.

So for you, it's not about paying out a lot of money, particularly in the preschool years. You can pay more, but that doesn't mean your child will receive lots of attention, affection, and real-live stimulation (as opposed to television or video games).

It takes an awful lot of time to find a good child care provider. You may not think you have that kind of time, but remember that this is one of the most important decisions you will make regarding both your child and your money.

If you decide on in-home care—either your house or the babysitter's (the path I chose)—many providers are willing to see you at their convenience after work or on weekends. While this may suit you for a longer interview, also ask permission to pop by during the week to meet any other children for whom she may provide care. If you choose a day care center, making time during the work week while they're open may be your only option.

PHOTOGRAPHIC MEMORY

One of my favorite memories is picking up my son at the end of the day and he doesn't want to leave until he's finished sweeping the babysitter's kitchen floor. He's wearing only a diaper and bare feet, and he's happily intent on his work.

DECISION FACTORS

Several factors are important to making your child care decision. One is knowing other families using the same provider. This is significant for many reasons. First, the single best way to find a good child care provider is through referrals, so ask everyone you know if they can refer someone, or if they know other families with children in day care with whom you can speak.

Another good reason to use the same provider as someone you know is because you are a single parent, and on those rare, and in some cases not so rare, situations when you can't make it on time to pick up your child, you need to line up backup resources. The easiest backup resource is someone who is already picking up a child at the same place, so both your child and the provider know this person.

You should offer to provide backup for other families as well.

If you live near your family, or in the same area where you grew up, you are likely to have a lot of backup resources. If you don't, making friends with the right sort of people you can trust with your child needs to be a top priority.

Reconcile Job and Child Care

I have not lived and raised my children near family members or areas where I grew up. While I have always lined up backup resources, very few days in my life, and I can probably count them on one hand, have I required an emergency backup to pick up my children from day care.

Again, am I the luckiest person on earth? Hardly. I have always made my children my top priority. This means, when I look for a job, I scope out whether or not a potential employer is the sort that will have a problem with my leaving at 5:00 p.m. every day in order to pick up my child on time.

I may not ask this question explicitly in the interview process, but I do ask about expectations regarding the workday. Specifically, I'll ask whether employee performance is measured by hours worked or the quality and timeliness of work. In every situation, the hiring manager I spoke with emphasized that they were not micromanagers and were only concerned with the quality of my work.

This didn't always turn out to be true. However, because I addressed this issue before I accepted the job, it was never a point of contention for me after that.

Single parents have to be there for their children. You can't call your husband or your wife and ask them to take their turn handling a situation. Even if you're divorced and there is another parent who can help out, consider them a backup resource. As a single parent, get used to being 100 percent responsible for your children. Organize your life in such a way that you have the flexibility to respond to unplanned situations.

If you choose to or currently work for an employer that does not provide you the necessary single parenting flexibility, start looking for a new one. When you find one, do not abuse your leverage for the privilege of flexibility. You have to do your part by working hard and delivering quality and timely work in order to preserve this leverage.

Sometimes you may feel like you have to work harder than your coworkers because of this. You have to cram all of your work into eight hours a day, while your coworkers can stretch it out and leisurely chat and socialize half the day because they can work longer hours or take work home.

If it helps, remember that you have someone waiting for you who will be excited to see you. You don't have to go home to an empty house and a frozen dinner. You have someone to cook for, and they'll eat it even if it's just sliced cucumbers and buttered pasta.

Also, remember that you don't have to plan your vacation around anyone else's schedule (other than your children's), visit in-laws, or visit a grumpy friend or college roommate you never liked. Remember that if you want to buy a blue couch, you don't have to settle for a red one.

There are trade-offs to every lifestyle. Single parents have some good ones, too.

FINDING CHILD CARE

Start by talking to everyone you know. You'd be surprised where some of the best leads come from.

I know of one mom who found a full-time babysitter by asking the teen-age babysitter of her neighbor's children. It turns out that the girl had a baby brother—the product of her mom's second marriage. Her mom had the option to be a stay-home mom this time around and was happy to take on a second child at a nominal fee.

HEAD OF HOUSEHOLD TIP: HOW TO FIND SITTERS

Talk to real estate agents familiar with people moving to and from your local area—they may be aware of who takes care of their clients' children and when there are openings. I found one of my sitters from an agent who was selling a house for clients moving out of town; my child took over their child's slot at the sitter's home.

Another option is to visit every religious institution in your town; church preschools are often less expensive than day care centers. Local YMCAs often have affordable child care as well. Many times, local Jewish Community Centers (JCC) enjoy a reputation for excellent child care supervision and facilities. Typically, YMCA and JCC will also consider reduced rates for lower-income families.

Sometimes, grandparents and other family members are eager to baby-sit for a small monetary fee. If you have a sibling, cousin, or aunt who is a stay-at-home mom, they may be willing to watch your child in return for you watching theirs on weekends or overnight. During the summer, you may be able to hire a college student or teacher who also has the summer off and is looking for income. This arrangement offers the flexibility of having someone who can drive and is not bound to a particular schedule. The babysitter can take your children to a neighborhood pool, extracurricular activities, birthday parties, or even run errands for you or themselves. This is a good option for older elementary or middle school children who need little supervision but whom you don't want to be at home alone all day. The ease and flexibility that this job offers should yield a lower cost than a regular day care center.

Consider sharing a nanny with another family to help ease the financial burden. The cost of a nanny per week is frequently equal to that of a day care, but if you can split the cost with another family, it may actually cost half as much. Plus, you have the added advantage of coming straight home instead of commuting to a day care center. You may even negotiate an extra hour or two a week to get your grocery shopping or errands done—something that is not an option at a day care center.

If you have the extra room, consider hiring a foreign au pair for discounted child care in exchange for room and board. Perhaps you can arrange for a further reduced discount if you allow her to care for an additional child or children in your home (she gets the additional child care income, you get a further reduced rate).

Check out local parenting magazines and journals, and not just for the articles and paid advertisements. Often there are classified ads in the back that announce county resources for on-site after-school programs or community service programs. This type of literature can often be found at your local library or is sent home from school in your child's backpack.

Some extracurricular programs now offer child care. An example: martial arts schools that pick up children after school in a van and take them back to the center for classes and supervised homework sessions.

Contact local elementary schools for tutors and retired school teachers who might be interested in preschool or after-school child care to help supplement their income.

HEAD OF HOUSEHOLD TIP: COMBINE CHILD CARE AND EXTRACURRICULAR ACTIVITIES

A good way to save both time and money is to combine your child care provider with your family club, such as a YMCA or a JCC. Regardless of your financial situation, it's important to recognize that—particularly for single parents—time is your most precious commodity.

Consider a child care option that also offers extracurricular classes that may interest your child, such as swimming lessons, dance, gymnastics, or martial arts. This is particularly important in the elementary school years for after-school care.

Sometimes the facility you choose for child care will also require that you be a member. One financial advantage is that you will then receive the member rate for any additional classes. When you combine child care with extracurricular activities, you can save your weekends. In other words, while your child is in after-school care, the counselors ensure he or she gets safely to and from his or her extracurricular class. Obviously, it's fun for your child and allows you to spend your Saturday morning doing something other than sitting in the waiting room of a karate or ballet school.

Always inquire about a single parent rate for club membership. Frequently you can get the single rate for both you and your family.

NIGHTTIME BABYSITTERS

Once you get full-time day care babysitting squared away, it's nice to line up an option or two for the occasions you want to go out.

Network with other single parents to find sitters or swap babysitting duties so neither of you have to pay out cash, and your children get playmates as a bonus.

Tap the teenage children of your friends. Or the friends of those teenagers. Ask the counselors at your preschool, day care, or summer camps if they ever do any extra babysitting outside of work (as long as this is allowed by the facility). Bear in mind that no one gets rich watching other people's children, so people in these professions are often seeking additional ways of earning income and child care is something that comes easy to them. The added bonus is that they already know your child, his likes and dislikes.

Most importantly, vet all sitter options. When you leave someone in your home with your child, you're leaving them with all of your most valued worldly possessions. Be absolutely sure you trust this person.

FUNDING CHILD CARE

Flexible Spending Arrangement

If your employer offers a dependent care flexible spending arrangement (FSA), consider using it to fund child care expenses. An FSA allows you to defer pretax money into an account to reimburse predictable child care expenses.

Initially, you benefit from reduced taxes on your take-home pay, much like a 401(k) deferral. But the real benefit is using untaxed income to reimburse child care expenses. As long as you estimate the correct amount for the year, you avoid paying taxes on all the money you pay on child care. Some employers even kick in a dollar or percentage match—in effect subsidizing some of your child care expenses.

The FSA dependent care account was formerly known as a Dependent Care Reimbursement Account (DCRA; called a "decra"). To reimburse expenses with a dependent care FSA, you must provide the tax ID or Social Security number of your child care provider. You determine a level amount that will come out of each paycheck and go into an account in your name. Then you have to pay your child care provider out of pocket, get a receipt, submit the receipt, and then you'll receive a reimbursement payment. This generally takes a bit of time, so you have to be able to pay your babysitter with less money from your paycheck, and then get the money back later. If you live paycheck to paycheck, this can squeeze you pretty tight.

However, one advantage is that once you get used to less money coming in from your paycheck, those periodic reimbursement checks seem like "free" money. Do something wise with them, like deposit them in a separate savings account earmarked to pay for next year's child care expenses. That way next year you won't even have to use your regular income for child care expenses and can contribute more to your 401(k) plan.

Because you have to submit receipts to be reimbursed from an FSA, you have to make the time and effort to do the paperwork. Another drawback to an FSA is that it is a "use it or lose it" account, meaning that whatever balance is left over at the end of the year you simply lose. If your child care situation is subject to change, projecting expenses a year in advance may be a bit of a challenge.

If you use a dependent care FSA, you are not able to claim your child care expenses as a tax deduction since the money you paid out was deducted from your paycheck before taxes. Unless your employer offers a monetary incentive, it may be easier to just claim the deduction on your taxes once a year and not bother with all the paperwork and worry about when you'll get reimbursed.

Child Care Tax Deduction

You may claim a child care deduction on your annual tax return, the maximum amount of which may vary year to year. This is a huge deduction advantage, even larger for head of household filers—which most single parents qualify to file as—and can result in a more substantial tax return.

Child Care Reimbursement

Some employers have begun offering child care tuition reimbursement. You may have to take the initiative and ask if yours does. Employers don't always promote their benefits for a couple of reasons. One is because it actually costs them money to offer them, so the less employees use them, the more the employer saves.

Second, as in the case of a child care reimbursement, they get in hot water by offering a benefit that not all employees can utilize. In this case, childless coworkers are unable to use the benefit. Of course, few single parents can stay after work and use the on-campus gym, but that's hardly the point.

Find out if your company offers a full or partial child care reimbursement, because the offer is entirely likely to be buried in the boundless forms and literature you received upon hire, and they won't tell you if you don't ask. Some such benefits are developed later and offered to new hires, though they may conveniently forget to inform incumbent employees.

When looking for new employment, try to find companies offering child care assistance with your benefits package. However, instead of asking directly and implying that *God Forbid* you have children, you may simply want to request their benefits literature.

Let Your Children Pay for Their Own Care

They can. That's because, by the very fact that you have children, enhanced by the very fact that you are a head of household tax filer, you are indeed likely to receive a hefty tax refund. Use this money to pay for next year's child care. If you are afraid you'll spend it before you need it, park it in a high-rate CD for three to six months and let it earn money for you.

Work from Home—Don't Need Child Care?

Take it from someone who works from home: Don't expect to get a lot of work done if you have a preschooler at home with you. It's better to get off-site child care for at least part of the day and learn to work eight hours in four (which is easy when no one distracts you).

FOUR

Credit

As a single parent, there may be times when you feel like your life is held together with duct tape and a bungee cord. Well, the same can be said for your credit. A good credit score is like duct tape: It can hold your financial life together when real money seems to slip from your grasp.

Good credit can mean the difference between buying and renting. It is the most important financial tool a single parent can develop for financial success. If you do nothing else well, take care of your credit score.

Treat your credit as if it's one of your children: Never ignore, abuse, or overindulge it. Consider your credit as one of your precious charges—pay it plenty of attention and recognize that it is a privilege to have as a responsibility, it is your path to success, and it can be your legacy for teaching good values (or the worst sort of financial values imaginable).

PERKS OF GOOD CREDIT

Your credit score can make a big difference in the types of interest rates you'll be offered. When shopping for a mortgage, there are three qualifying factors used to determine interest rates: Your credit history, the amount of your down payment, and your current income. If your credit rating is less than perfect, you'll need to fare extremely well in the other two categories.

YOUR CREDIT REPORT

Your credit report contains a numerical score that takes into account several factors. In recent years, the following are the most influential factors that impact your credit score.

1. Payment Record

- Whether or not you've made payments on time.
- If you have some late payments, it matters what type of accounts you paid late.

An installment loan account is where you borrow a set amount and then repay it over time, such as primary mortgages and car loans. A revolving debt account is where you have a line of credit that you can borrow against, repay some or all of it, and continue borrowing against up to a limit. Examples include credit cards and home equity lines of credit. In terms of credit scoring, installment loans are preferable to revolving debt.

- It matters as to how late your payments are.
- The actual amount(s) you still owe is a factor.
- The number of accounts you have matters.

2. Present Obligations

- The total amount you owe should be less than 50 percent (preferably 30% or less; optimally 10% or less) of the amount of credit available to you.
- The types of accounts to which you owe matter. A home mortgage (installment loan) is considered good credit. Credit cards (revolving debt), not so much.
- The number of your accounts that carry balances matter, but there is merit to spreading out your debt among cards because "maxing out" cards can result in lower scoring.

It is important that you continue to actively use your credit, as this is the only way to develop a good track record for paying back your debts. Even if you don't need to, use your credit cards now and then to keep them actively tracked in your credit report. If you never use credit, you will end up with a low score.

It is equally important to stay current on your bills. Even if you just pay minimums to stay current, this is very important. Even if it takes a lifetime to pay off your debt, you can still maintain a good credit score by staying current.

If you miss a couple of payments but then make a big payment, or even pay off a card, this will still hurt your credit score. *Don't miss payments.*

3. History and Activity

- The longer you hold your credit accounts, the better. Don't close them just because they're old.
- The average age of all your accounts matters. The older ones help offset the impact of opening a new account once in awhile.
- Activity is good. Rotate the cards you use and pay diligently so each gets used once in awhile.
- Applying for new credit can lower your score, so make sure you research the best account for your needs and don't apply for new credit precipitously.
- Making requests for credit limit increases should also be done sparingly.

"Hard inquiries" come from creditors checking your score based on your request for new or more credit. You lose score points from hard inquiries.

Less damaging are "soft inquiries," which are inquiries from you checking your own credit, employers or prospective employers checking your credit, insurance company inquiries, and creditors that want to send you "preapproved" promotional offers.

- Trends in payment patterns are significant, like whether you always pay on time or how often you miss.
- Obviously, any bankruptcies, judgments, suits, liens, wage attachments, or collection items will drop your score. The most important factor is how recently these events occurred, and your payment track record since then.
- Any negative information will remain on your report for up to 7 years; bankruptcy will continue to be reported for 10 years.

With the latest versions of the FICO scoring model, the number of credit cards a consumer holds is no longer a factor in the score calculation the way it used to be. Your income and bank balances are not tracked in your credit report and not factored into your credit score. Nor are the interest rates you pay on your accounts.

TIPS FOR DEVELOPING GOOD CREDIT

- Pay on time; how much you pay isn't as important as how timely you pay it.
- Use credit cards sparingly, but do use them.

If you're adamant about paying cash, alleviate this situation by writing a check for the amount of each credit card purchase you make whenever you get home. Put these checks in a drawer, and then mail them out when your credit card bill comes in at the end of the month. Most cards provide a grace period between the time you make a purchase and the time it starts charging you interest—typically about 20–25 days. This may seem like a useless exercise, but it's a way to build a good credit history while learning to stay within your monthly budget.

Another option is to use an online banking account to set up your credit card vendors and pay off the charged amounts whenever you get home, without waiting for the bill.

- Steer clear of retail store cards, which tend to have higher interest rates and lower credit limits.
- Don't cancel cards you don't use (with the exception of retail store cards), as you essentially reduce the amount of your available credit and make any balances you carry a higher percentage of credit utilization.
- Don't apply for credit you don't need—each inquiry stays on your record, indicating you either want too much or have been turned down too often.
- The more you shop around, the more it hurts your credit score. For example, if you apply with one of the online mortgage companies that shops rates for you, each time one of these companies or their partners pulls your credit report, your credit rating drops by about four points. Shopping and research is fine, but don't fill out an application until you're really serious about making a purchase.

ERRORS ON YOUR CREDIT REPORT

Credit reports are widely acknowledged to contain errors, particularly for people with common names. That's why it's a good idea to check your credit report periodically. The easiest way to do this is to go to www .annualcreditreport.com.

This central site allows you to request a free credit report once every 12 months from each of the nationwide consumer credit reporting companies: Equifax, Experian, and TransUnion.

If you find discrepancies, use the form provided to detail the items you want to dispute and send it back to the credit bureau from where you requested the report. It's the bureau's job to investigate your claim with creditors and determine if the item should be removed.

The credit bureau is required to resolve the issue within 30 days or remove it temporarily until the issue is resolved. Creditors must prove that disputed information is accurate before it will be reinserted into your report. If you still disagree with the report, you're allowed to submit a statement regarding the issue that will accompany every report sent out thereafter.

However, if it's not a mistake, it's not going to come off your record. It can take a long time to clear up problems on a credit report, so if you're in the market for a car loan or mortgage, be sure to get a copy of your report three to six months before starting the process.

DIVORCED CREDIT

In a divorce situation, there is often a huge problem with shared debt— and how to get out from under an ex-spouse's credit rating. Many times one spouse will have a poor credit rating due to his or her ex-spouse's spending habits. You can divorce your other half, but not necessarily the damage to your credit report.

Both spouses are liable for outstanding balances on all joint accounts, even after divorce. However, you can ask creditors to close joint accounts and convert or reopen these as individual accounts. Even if you revert to using your maiden name after a divorce, credit problems will resurface when you apply for a mortgage.

By the same token, if your credit rating when you were married was good, have the credit bureau transfer old account information to a file under your new name. By law, lenders must recognize that credit established with an ex-spouse is shared credit.

Time heals all wounds, including broken marriages and injuries to your credit. Credit problems from the past can often be overlooked if you reestablish good credit since then. Clean up credit issues, pay all of your bills on time, then wait six months to a year to apply for new credit sources, such as a mortgage or car loan.

STRATEGIES FOR PAYING OFF CREDIT CARDS

Rule Number One: There's only one way to get out from under a mound of credit card debt, and that's to stop using your credit cards or pay them off in full every month. Rule Number Two: If you're not willing to follow rule number one, nothing else will work.

Now that we've got the traditional rules out of the way, relax a bit and appreciate the fact that since single parents don't live a traditional lifestyle, the traditional rules don't always apply to single parents. The reality is that credit is your lifeboat; your saving grace when it's two weeks till Christmas and you just lost your job and there is no other money coming in to buy your children presents.

Credit is your friend. Treat it well, and it will always be there for you.

Because single parents can't always live by the traditional rules, you're more likely to fall into the eternal black hole of debt. You're not alone; you're in fine company. Plenty of single and married folks do as well, so it's not a plight exclusive to single parents. It's just one that is very common when you have only one income and more than one mouth to feed, clothe, house, insure, drive, and gift.

If you are resolute about getting out of debt—a particularly good New Year's Resolution to make—follow this plan and see where you stand at the end of the next year.

- Create four columns on a sheet of paper. Under column one, list all of your creditors to whom you owe money. In column two, detail the amounts you owe for each. In column three, put down the interest rate each creditor charges. And in column four, the minimum payment for that creditor.

- Prioritize your list so that the creditor who charges the highest interest rate comes first, and list the others in descending interest rate order, regardless of the balances you owe.

- Each month, pay your minimums to each creditor, and apply all excess money you have to the first creditor on your list. Your goal is to tackle the highest interest rate creditor first, and then work your way down. In the end, this will save you the most money.

For example, let's say you have budgeted as much as $400 toward your credit card debt each month (see Table C). Pay the minimums to your lowest interest rate cards and then apply the excess, up to your $400 limit, to your highest interest rate card. In the scenario detailed in Table C, you

Table C   Credit Worksheet

Credit card	Balance owed ($)	Interest rate (%)	Minimum payment ($)
Credit card #1	4,500.00	15.99	135.00
Credit card #2	2,500.00	12.49	75.00
Credit card #3	3,075.00	10.99	92.00
Credit card #4	800.00	6.99	25.00
Total monthly minimum			**327.00**

would pay $208 to Credit card #1 ($135 minimum plus the difference between the $400 you can afford and the $327 already committed).

Once you've paid off one credit card balance, use the money you were paying to increase your payment on the next highest interest rate balance. In this example, you would then be able to throw $283 at your next highest interest rate card, which will pay off much quicker than at the $75 a month pace you were paying. And so on.

If possible, transfer credit card balances to a card with a lower fixed interest rate and use the subsequent savings to help further pay off the balance. Make sure that the interest rate is low enough to warrant any onetime transfer fees you incur (usually 2–4% of the amount transferred).

Thou Shalt Resist Teenage Peer Pressure

There is nothing more irresistible than an empty credit card for which you've finally paid off the balance. You feel so good about yourself that you want to treat your loving teenage daughter, who came home from school all chatty and excited today. She informs you that she can't live without that two-week trip to France with the French Club next summer. And it would only cost $2,000, which you realize you could charge to that waiting and wanting credit card you just paid off. Excusez-moi?

During those two weeks her friends are away on the coveted trip, serve French bread with Brie and fill the house with French music and language lessons you check out from the local library. Buy her a secondhand beret from a vintage store. She'll get over it.

HEAD OF HOUSEHOLD "GET OUT OF DEBT CHECKLIST"

✓ Make a complete list of your assets, debts, monthly expenses, and monthly disposable income. Track your debt reduction each month.

✓ Limit the amount of credit you use—pay off one card before you use another.

✓ Don't apply for credit you don't need—each inquiry stays on your record, indicating you either want too much or have been turned down too often.

✓ Brainstorm ways to cut expenses, which may be as painful as giving up cable TV and/or Internet access. Get your children involved. It will help them learn to live on a budget early on, and simply making them more aware of daily expenses won't scar them for life.

✓ Pay an extra $10–15 toward your debt whenever you can.

✓ Pay your bills on time, even if you only make minimum payments. Many people think it is okay to skip a month and then make a double payment the next month. That's not how it works, and those blemishes will show up on your credit report.

✓ Contact your creditors and ask for assistance. Be prepared to share your budget with them and commit to a monthly payment.

✓ If you are unable to negotiate lower interest rates or payments on your own, contact a credit counseling service to do this on your behalf. Many legitimate credit counseling services are nonprofit organizations and do not charge or offer this service at a nominal fee. However, you should be aware that working with one of these services may show up as a negative mark on your credit report if they arrange for you to pay below-market interest rates and monthly payments.

BORROW MONEY TO CONSOLIDATE DEBT

Using credit isn't the crime—paying high interest rates is. If you own a home, consider taking out a home equity loan (also known as a second mortgage) or line of credit to pay off your credit cards. These loans normally charge a much lower interest rate than credit cards and the amount you pay in interest is tax deductible.

However, a home equity loan puts your home at risk should you default on your payments. Consider this risk very carefully. It's one thing to have to declare bankruptcy; it's something altogether different to be both bankrupt and homeless. Not to mention that being homeless could cause you to lose custody of your children.

Another option is to consider applying for a personal loan at your bank. Often the rates offered on personal loans run lower than credit cards, and this may allow you to consolidate your credit card debt into one monthly payment at a lower rate.

TRANSFER HIGH-RATE BALANCES

If you take good care of your credit, you will likely receive offers from yours or other prospecting credit card companies guaranteeing you a low, low interest rate if you open a new account and transfer your current balances to their credit card.

Be careful and read the fine print. Many of those promotions only offer that rate for six months or less, and then convert to some gargantuan rate that may well be higher than what you're currently paying. Unless you are currently in dire circumstances, ignore those offers.

The offer you want to accept is the lowest rate possible for the life of the balance transferred. The rates offered can vary, but during some economic environments, can go as low as 2.99 percent or less. A rate that low is worth considering even for other big-ticket purchases, such as a car. Many times credit card offers will offer a lower rate than car loans for the balance of the loan—*if you have a good credit score.*

However, the fine print will tell you that you must always make the minimum monthly payment, at very least, before the due date. Otherwise, the deal is off and you'll get pushed into some other ridiculous interest rate bracket.

Here are the most important things to remember about balance transfers:

- Any balance currently on the card will not receive the new low rate for life. Not only that, but the current balance might be the last your payments end up touching, so you may continue to accrue interest at the previous higher rate while you pay down the newly transferred amount at the lower rate.

- Because of this, it's important to take advantage of a low rate for lifetime of balance on a card that does not already have a balance (unless the current balance is enjoying the same or lower rate for its lifetime).

- Once you've made a balance transfer to a card, stop using that card. Any new purchases will likely incur a higher purchase rate and you may accrue interest at that higher rate while you pay down the lower rate on the transferred amount.

Every credit card is different, even those offered by the same company. Before you jump at one of these deals, read the literature carefully and get answers to all of the following questions before you take advantage of a credit card offer:

- Will you be charged a processing or transfer fee for transferring each of your balances from other cards?
- Is there a minimum or maximum cap for this fee?
- Does this card require that you close the accounts from which you transfer balances, and do you really want to do that? (Remember, closing accounts will drive your "maxing out" percentage rate even higher.)
- Does the interest rate increase if you are ever a day late with a payment? By how much?
- When the interest rate offered on your balance transfer expires, what will the new rate be?
- Can you use a balance transfer offer to write a check to yourself and deposit it in your bank account in order to consolidate other bills such as medical bills and other small loans? Is this a good strategy for you over the long term?

PAY LATE OR MISS A PAYMENT?

As a general rule, most lenders don't take collection action until a payment is at least five days overdue, which allows for any mailing snafus. And in most cases, a lender is not likely to repossess your car after one missed payment. After all, he doesn't want your car, he wants the money you owe him.

There are two things you should know if you are ever in this situation:

1. If you know you have to miss a payment, call and try to negotiate a new due date beforehand. Your car may not be repossessed after one missed payment, but your credit may take a hit.

Take this precaution because your credit—believe it or not—is more important than your car.

2. Know that you have much more leeway to solve your payment problems with a creditor *before* you miss a payment, as you are proactively demonstrating responsibility.

A strong, consistent payment track record is as good as gold when it comes to negotiating. Say, for instance, you took advantage of a 3.99 percent interest rate for the life of a balance transfer with a credit card you've held responsibly for years. Then one month you're late on a payment. Call the company immediately, explain why your payment is late, and ask them not to change the 3.99 percent for life rate to the enormous default rate due to a late payment. With a strong payment history, they may be willing to forgo the rate increase for your one transgression.

If you don't call before or after you miss a payment, your lender's actions may vary depending on your past payment history. Your lender may wait anywhere from 10 to 20 days before giving you a phone call. If you have a strong track record, the missed payment may just show up on your next bill with a penalty fee. This is one of the many, many reasons having good credit can make your life easier.

Your best action is to call your lender as soon as you know you're going to miss a payment. Your lender may be able to offer options, such as

- Change Due Date—Your lender may agree to permanently change the date your payment is due each month. For example, perhaps it would be better to make this payment after your second paycheck of each month instead of the first.
- Deferment—One or two missed payments can be tacked onto the back end of your loan so that your delinquency is temporarily forgiven but your loan is extended by the payments and subsequent interest charged.
- Government Programs—Your lender may be aware of government programs that can help you out during hard times. For example, military service members may apply for a reduced interest rate on mortgage payments or credit card debt, thanks to the Soldiers' and Sailors' Civil Relief Act.

One of the first things to do when you know you're in trouble is reread your lender's contract. Your contract will typically outline a schedule of what will happen when payments are missed, ranging from late fees to repossession. This simple act of reading your contract may motivate you to pick up the phone and work to save your credit.

While you need to know what the contract has bound you to, keep in mind that this is a starting point for negotiation. More than anything, your creditor wants you to keep making your payments. It costs him money to repossess, auction, or take you to court. If you have a good payment record with your lender up to this point, you will likely find him flexible with arrangements until you're back in good shape.

Should your payments get behind by 60–90 days, you can expect trouble. The lender escalation process starts with a couple of reminder calls, then a couple of letters, and then a deficiency notification.

In the case of a car loan, a letter of deficiency is the last step before repossession. In this letter, your lender will outline exactly what you must do to retain your car. If your car gets repossessed, it may be sold at an auction to the highest bidder.

This is not the worst of it.

If the lender does not recoup the loan's remaining balance through the sale of the car, you are still responsible for the outstanding amount. In fact, the lender may file a lawsuit to obtain a deficiency judgment against you, which translates into another bad mark on your credit report.

Most lenders report borrower information on a monthly basis, so even one payment over 30 days past due is likely to affect your score. And delinquent payments 60–90 days past due will remain on your credit record for up to seven years.

This type of negative reporting can seriously hamper your ability to obtain credit in the future. You'll likely be offered higher interest rates or may be turned down altogether.

So: You lose your car, you still owe the money, and your credit score drops so you can't get a loan for a new one. Bear in mind that it's a whole lot easier to manage debt on the front end rather than suffer the consequences of the back end.

DEBT COUNSELING/CREDIT REPAIR

Dealing with debt can be mind boggling, and most people just put off having to figure out what to do indefinitely. This is the worst thing you can do, because time is your worst enemy when it comes to compounding interest rates. Even if you stop charging new purchases to your credit cards, continuing to make minimum payments can be like digging a hole in the surf. Your debt will continue to escalate due to high interest rates.

If you are considering the services and advice of a professional debt counselor, bear in mind that no one can legally remove accurate and timely negative information from a credit report. This includes the credit repair agencies you see on late-night TV. You (or a company you pay) can dispute a charge on your credit report, but if the charge is legitimate, it will appear again on the report after 45 days. Many companies simply take your money and show you that the claim is removed from the report. Don't be surprised when it shows back up a couple of months after you paid to "have it removed."

There are two types of debt assistance: debt counseling/management, and debt negotiation/settlement. Seek out the services of debt counseling/management, as these agencies should be registered as a 501-C-3 nonprofit agency. A trained and certified counselor at this type of agency can offer you budget and debt-management counseling or classes, and help you develop a personalized plan to help solve your credit issues now and avoid them in the future. In fact, current legislation requires that you receive this type of credit counseling and attend a debtor education course before and after you file for personal bankruptcy. Your counselor should be able to assess your eligibility for a debt-management program (DMP). A DMP requires that you deposit money in an account with the credit agency to pay your outstanding credit card bills, student loans, and medical bills according to a payment schedule negotiated between you and your creditors. A DMP generally takes up to four years to complete, but your credit score is likely to increase at the end of the plan.

The DMP is basically a disciplined plan designed to help you pay debt that you have accrued, preferably at lower interest rates and devoid of penalties. Payment for this type of service should be nominal, around $50 or less than $25 a month if you set up a DMP.

However, you want to avoid the second type of debt assistance, that of a debt negotiation or settlement agency. The goal of the debt settlement agency (which may also be registered as a 501-C-3 nonprofit agency, so don't make this your only guide) is to negotiate payment for a percentage of your actual debt.

This is bad for many reasons. First of all, it requires that your creditor(s) forgive a percentage of your debt, so you don't take the responsibility of paying off money you borrowed. That's like a get-out-of-jail-free card when you actually committed the crime, and it most certainly is not a good value to pass on to your children.

The financial aspects, however, are bad too. Whatever amount (over $600) is forgiven is reported to the IRS and you have to pay taxes on it as if it was earned income. Your credit report will receive a bad mark indicating that the debt was "paid as settled" instead of "paid in full," and that's a "tell" to future creditors with whom you may seek credit. This negative mark stays on your credit report for seven years.

The worse part though is that you may not get your debt paid and could even end up worse than where you started. While you send monthly payments to the agency to help pay off your debt, they may not make these payments. Instead, they collect the money until one of your credit accounts goes into default, and then use the money to negotiate a lower payoff on that one account. Meanwhile, all your other accounts may continue to report delinquency and accrue exorbitant fees and penalties.

Debt negotiation agencies also tend to charge higher fees than debt management agencies. They typically also receive a kickback from creditors in exchange for facilitating payment on delinquent accounts.

All in all, a bad idea. If you do feel the need to seek debt assistance, do so carefully and consider the following examples of poor advice you may receive from an agency that claims it can "fix" your credit situation:

- You are not informed of your rights and what you can do for yourself for free.
- The counselor recommends that you do not contact any of the three major national credit reporting companies directly.
- The service claims it can get rid of most or all the negative credit information in your credit report (even if that information is accurate and current).
- The company suggests that you apply for an Employer Identification Number (EIN) to use instead of your Social Security number in order to reinvent a "new" credit identity and subsequent credit report. By the way, applying for an EIN under false pretenses is a federal crime.

Should you engage one of these services, be mindful never to pay for credit repair services before they are provided, even if you are pressured to do so. Under the Credit Repair Organizations Act, credit repair companies cannot require you to pay until they have completed the services they have promised.

Here's the final thing to remember: Establishing a strong credit score is not about avoiding debt or getting out of debt; it's about maintaining smart debt.

FIVE

Health

Health care is a no-skimp zone for single parents. If you've got strong backup resources to help run your household when you get sick, that's great. But either way, here's some good advice for single parents:

- Don't get sick;
- If you get sick, take every precaution to get better soon;
- Always maintain good health insurance for you and your children.

DON'T GET SICK

Well this just sounds ridiculous, but bear in mind that an ill parent in a single parent household means total breakdown of life as we know it. Laundry doesn't get done. Sticky things must lay wait on the floor. Television becomes an acceptable form of 24/7 entertainment. Pets often go unattended.

HEAD OF HOUSEHOLD TIP: KIDS AND PETS

Where pets are concerned, don't give in to getting one until you are completely confident that your child is old enough to feed and, if necessary, walk it by himself. Don't think for a moment that he or she will actually do this on a regular basis; more likely it will fall to you, or at least the nagging part. There is nothing more fun than having a stare-down with your dog by his empty bowl every night trying to figure out if he's been fed because your child can't remember and your dog lies. The point is just ensure your child is old enough to take over when you get sick.

When the single parent goes down sick, meals become cereal, popcorn, and ice cream—all decent nutritional sources so long as it doesn't go on forever.

> **HEAD OF HOUSEHOLD TIP: TEACH THEM TO FIX MEALS**
>
> One of the first rules of thumb as a single parent is to teach your children how to fix food for themselves, as early as possible. Any two-year-old can eat dry cereal out of the box. The microwave is a single parent's best friend (and uses less energy than a stove). Keep single serve ice cream cups on hand.

Do take desperate measures not to get sick. The whole hand-washing, flu shot, and don't take unnecessary leg-breaking risks come into play here. Mortality and disability are things single parents need to consider all the time, more so than the average adult population.

That's because if you die, your child will become an orphan (even if she has relatives to go to, she'll still be a parentless child). Or, if you're divorced, you have to worry that if you die, your child may likely go live full-time with your ex. In some cases, that may be even scarier.

Stay healthy. Naturally, that means *regular exercise* and *eating well*, and these two things thankfully do not require a lot of money to accomplish. This is not only to avoid sickness or an unhealthy weight, but these factors are also two of the top three most important values you can pass on to your children (the third being *money management*).

If educational curricula, from preschool up through college, would focus on nutrition and financial management, we would all be a lot better off. A minimum of one year in each subject should be requisite for junior high, high school, and college matriculation.

> **HEAD OF HOUSEHOLD TIPS: GOOD HEALTH**
>
> • When you feel overwhelmed, cry. Biologically speaking, tears release protein-based hormones that are produced by our body when under stress. Crying allows you to excrete these hormones, and actually makes you feel better. Interesting to note, however, that these hormones are not as prevalent in tears produced by irritants, such as cutting onions or exposure to allergens (just goes to show that you can't fake a good cry). Crying isn't a weakness; it's an empowerment to help you feel better and more confident.

- Walk for fun. Walking can create some of the best times and memories with your children—they get your complete attention and you can observe things together outside. Make it a nightly habit. If you have a dog he can walk with you, it's a full family bonding experience.

- As much as possible, shop only the outer perimeter of the grocery store. That's where all the healthier fare from the basic food groups lie; it's the prepackaged and processed stuff that's in the aisles.

Germ Exposure to Build a Strong Immune System

Okay, I've got one disclaimer for this discussion. In my experience, the people most vulnerable to illness often seem to be those most conscientious about prevention. I call them the "Hand Washers." You can find them in the bathroom at work washing their hands for a whole minute, then using a sleeve on the door handle to exit to avoid picking up germs. Not a bad idea, it's just that they appear to be the same people who take loads of vitamin supplements, make complicated "on the side" orders at restaurants, and lo and behold, seem to get sick more often than those of us who surreptitiously reuse steak knives that have dropped on the floor. I have a theory that germ exposure, within reason, can actually help build the immune system. In other words, the "three-second rule" for eating off the floor may well prevent many common illnesses. (In our house, we've revised the rule to simply, "eat it before the dog gets it"—typically longer than three seconds because the dog's not that fond of my cooking.) It's not a proven theory, of course, merely my experience. But my children don't tend to get sick very often, so I'm sticking with it.

TAKE EVERY PRECAUTION TO GET BETTER SOON

So, as a single parent, it's important that you don't get sick. But what if you do?

Stay home. That's what sick days are for. People who insist on going to work with a horrific cough or messy sneezes are apparently more important than anyone else who may catch their illness and subsequently miss work.

Be considerate, of yourself, your children, other people with whom you might come in contact, their children, their children's schoolmates and teachers, their spouses, and all the people their spouses work with.

Don't become a Typhoid Mary, and don't let your child become one either.

If you're sick for more than two days, go see a doctor. Single parents cannot afford to be sick more than two or three days, and this has nothing to do with money. This has to do with the survival of a clean and efficient household. If you wait any longer, you'll get sick again looking at the mess you have to clean up.

What this has to do with money is that a simple illness can become a much bigger illness because you don't take care of yourself (or your child) at the outset. Consider bed rest and/or a visit to the doctor—a small investment that will save you money down the line.

In other words, prevent the flu from becoming pneumonia, which sends one in four people who get it to the hospital each year. It is also the eighth leading cause of death in the United States.

MAINTAIN GOOD HEALTH INSURANCE

Health care expenses have risen to the point of insanity in recent years. Employers are doing everything they can to pass that burden on to their employees by paying out less and setting expectations for good health. In other words, the healthier the employee, the more expense an employee will pick up—or pay out to you as an incentive.

Not a bad idea, as far as incentives go, but you really shouldn't rely on your employer to tell you to exercise and eat right. Especially when you hear this message in one ear and yet hear muted undertones that you should work through lunch in the other.

The fact is health insurance plans are very complicated. If you work for a larger employer, you'll probably be offered several options, and it can feel like a tremendous burden to try and figure out the best one for your family—both in coverage and cost.

However, dig in one evening, study everything you received and even go online to research your options. The thing is once you make this type of analysis, it gets easier the next time. You know what to look for, what questions to ask, you'll learn the terms and the traps and be able to weigh your past coverage against what you'd like better in the future.

HEAD OF HOUSEHOLD TIP: ENJOY WHAT'S GOOD

One of the perks of single parenting is that your insurance expense is for only one adult. Adult insurance is typically more expensive than children's. So in other words, your tab may be less for a family of three consisting of you and two children than for another family of three consisting of two parents and one child. *Yay for the little things.*

FOUR TYPES OF COVERAGE

Every type of health care insurance plan is different. Many insurers offer employers an à la carte menu so they can pick and choose the types of benefits they want to offer their workforce, and then you may have a smattering of options to choose from. Having lots of options may make it confusing, but it also allows you to customize a plan that better suits the needs of your family.

In other words, if you and your children are generally in good heath, you may opt for a lower cost plan. Drug coverage is typically more expensive, and therefore, better suited for families with one or more members who have ongoing prescriptions. If you're prone to need only prescribed medications for the infrequent times you get sick, this coverage may not be as meaningful for you. It may be more cost effective to keep your premiums low and pay more for prescriptions on an as-needed basis.

The following is a primer to help you understand general nuances. You really have to dig into the literature and online resources of each plan you are offered to make a needs-versus-cost evaluation specific to your family.

1. **Traditional Health Insurance Coverage**

Traditional insurance coverage—the kind people had back before all the bells and whistles—covers most of your health care bills, but not all of them. It may pay out a percentage of each bill, such as 80 percent, while you're responsible for the remaining 20 percent.

Traditional insurance may or may not cover preventive care such as well-child visits and physical exams, mammograms, and pap smears. Generally, the more coverage, the higher the premium.

Traditional plans may also require a deductible, meaning that you have to pay a certain amount out of pocket before coverage kicks in. An advantage of many traditional insurance plans is that you may see any doctor or hospital you want. A disadvantage is that the monthly premium can be higher than that of other types of health care insurance plans.

2. **Health Maintenance Organization (HMO)**

HMO plans typically cover most health care bills such as annual checkups, office visits, and even hospitalization. Many or all of these services will require a small co-payment anywhere from $5 to $40 or higher in some cases. One advantage to HMOs is that monthly premiums tend to be lower. A disadvantage with many HMOs is that you may be required to use only doctors and hospitals affiliated with your HMO, and you may have to obtain authorization for certain services and referrals to specialists. A searchable directory of affiliated physicians can usually be found at the HMO's Web site.

3. **Preferred Provider Organization (PPO)**

A PPO prefers that you choose your health care provider from its pre-ferred list (with whom it has negotiated lower rates). However, a PPO generally gives you the option to go to a provider not on its list, but you may have to pay out a greater portion of the cost. You may have to fork up a co-pay for some services; you may have deductible with your plan; and in some cases, you may have to file a claim form.

4. **Point of Service (POS)**

With a POS plan, you have the greatest degree of choice in exchange for a potentially greater cost. You can use the plan like an HMO and see "in-network" providers (physicians and medical facilities). Your services will generally be covered. However, if you want to choose an "out-of-network" physician for a specific issue, you have that option and your coverage will work like a traditional plan in which you are responsible for a deductible and a percentage of your bill. This may be a good option if you anticipate that general HMO care will be more than sufficient for part of your family, but one person may need more specialized care or prefers a doctor who is not part of the HMO.

The following are questions you should ask to help you evaluate the best health care plan for your family:

- Are the doctors, hospitals, and other providers you prefer covered as "in-network" or "out-of-network" under the plan?
- What is the coverage for services within the plan's network?
- What is the coverage for services out of the plan's network?
- With an HMO, are there enough doctors with different specialties and are they located conveniently to you?
- Are any services covered 100 percent (such as preventive care)?
- Do these services require a co-pay?
- Is there a deductible? Is it different for you versus your family?
- If so, can you adjust it to lower the premium that you pay?
- What is the co-pay for a primary care physician visit? Specialist visit?
- Are all prescriptions covered? Are some covered and some not (which ones)?
- How much coverage is provided for prescriptions? (Sometimes there are tiers—some medications get more coverage than others; this may be detailed on the insurer's Web site—called a drug formulary.)
- Is there an annual cap on out-of-pocket expenses in a year?

- Is there an annual maximum benefit?
- How difficult is it to see a specialist or get a second opinion? Would you need a referral?
- Does the plan cover extras such as eye care or chiropractic visits?

There is a lot to consider with health insurance, not the least of which is the general health and ages of members of your family. Children under five tend to get sick more often and require office visits.

Allergies or asthma, once diagnosed, remains a stickler for higher premiums even if children grow out of it or have mild cases.

Some smaller employers will offer only one type of health coverage plan, and it may be expensive. Before you commit to this coverage, do your own shopping for individual health care coverage to compare prices and coverage options.

FLEXIBLE SPENDING ARRANGEMENT

Like the Dependent Care FSA (see Chapter 3), many employers offer a health care flexible spending arrangement (FSA; a.k.a. Health Care Reimbursement Account, HCRA, or "hecra") so that you can pay predictable health care expenses with tax-free income.

Health care FSAs require a very accurate degree of predictability. You may set aside a certain amount of money from your pretaxed salary to go into a health care FSA for out-of-pocket medical expenses not covered by your insurance.

As you pay off medical bills, you send in the requisite paperwork to the plan provider and, in return, receive a check from your flex account reimbursing your expenses. However, the biggest caveat to a health care FSA is that it is a "use it or lose it" account—whatever money you don't use by the end of the year is forfeited. That's a problem if you don't plan well.

However, if you know you're going to pay a set orthodontia bill every month for the next two years, an FSA can help you pay for braces with tax-free money. Same for birth control pills and other medication that you must pay for and take on a monthly basis.

Once predetermined at the beginning of your employer's plan year, you can't alter the amount of money you contribute from your paycheck each month—even if your child gets his or her braces off early. However, you can use the money for any other qualified expenses, so you may want to stock up on contacts or prescription drugs if you've still got money left in the account at the end of the year.

Better yet, an FSA has exceedingly more generous qualifying expenses than your basic health insurance plan may cover. Things like acupuncture and stop-smoking programs and chiropractors and psychiatric care. Plus, an employee may request reimbursement for children's health care expenses, as well as his own.

FSAs are becoming more utilized due to the growing popularity of non-conventional treatment plans and alternative medicine. In addition, employees are beginning to recognize that FSAs offer more flexibility and greater opportunity to actually use the money they would normally sink into vision and dental care insurance premiums.

A TAX-ADVANTAGED EXAMPLE

Say, for example, you set aside $2,000 per year in a health care FSA. You use the money to reimburse payments for your family's medical expenses, including routine dental exams, four cavity fillings, an emergency root canal, your son's wisdom teeth, your daughter's contacts, back-to-school physical co-pays, and additional screenings.

Assuming your salary is taxed at 25¢ out of each dollar, only 75¢ per dollar is left to pay uncovered medical expenses. With a flex plan, each full dollar is available to reimburse qualified expenses. In this scenario, if you use the full $2,000 deferred to your health care account, you will save roughly $500 in taxes. You will also reduce your current taxes on each paycheck, similar to the way a 401(k) contribution works, as the money contributed to the FSA is transferred out before income taxes are applied.

HEALTH REIMBURSEMENT ARRANGEMENT

A health reimbursement arrangement (HRA) is an account that only your employer funds—you as an employee do not contribute. You may receive a tax-free reimbursement on qualified medical expenses you pay for up to a maximum dollar amount for a coverage period.

INDIVIDUAL PLANS

Thanks to today's online resources, you can comparison shop for health insurance all in one place. Conduct a search for "health insurance premium comparison" and then let one of the sites do all the work.

Once you answer a smattering of questions specific to you and your family's circumstances, you may receive a comparison of benefits and price quotes which you may then adjust by tweaking benefits.

The health insurance industry is very aware of rising heath care costs over the last decade and continues to devise ways to cut costs and increase value. Couple this phenomenon with the wave of people now pursuing independent careers (due to downsizing or out of sheer frustration of working for corporate America), and you may discover that you can actually get an individual health insurance policy for less than you'd pay for an employer plan.

Better yet, some employers will pay you for waiving health insurance under their plan, paying you the money they save by not subsidizing your health insurance. An added bonus to securing an individual plan is that you can maintain continuity in your insurance even if you decide to change jobs.

For healthy families, consider a traditional plan with a high out-of-pocket deductible. Many of these plans offer 100 percent coverage for annual checkups, immunizations, and regular screenings. If you and your family do not often get sick, you may benefit from paying a much lower premium. The higher the deductible you select, the lower the monthly premium.

If you do have a bad year in terms of health, take advantage of meeting your deductible. Fill up on prescriptions, visit a dermatologist for mole checks or any other type of health care pursuits that you might normally forgo. You may even consider having a surgery you've been putting off. Once you've hit your deductible, additional covered services may be 100 percent covered or a percentage of their costs (as with an 80%/ 20% plan).

It may be an expensive year in terms of health care, but much cheaper than if you were to pay a full deductible and/or 100 percent of expenses year after year. If you find you're paying out more than you can afford in health care each year, it may be time to shop for an HMO or lower cost plan.

HEALTH SAVINGS ACCOUNT

One of the newest developments in recent years is the HSA—a tax-advantaged health savings account that may be opened in concert with a high-deductible health care plan. Some employers may offer these, and even contribute money toward them as part of your health care insurance subsidy.

However, this combination of policy + HSA is also available to independent contractors and sole proprietor entrepreneurs. If you work for yourself, consider procuring a high-deductible health care plan (HDHP) and opening an accompanying HSA. While you may not receive an employer subsidy, this combination can keep your out-of-pocket health care expenses down while providing some pretty meaty tax advantages.

Basically, you pay your health care premiums out of your own pocket. Recently, this expense has also become tax deductible for self-employed individuals. Yay.

Next, you contribute as much (or as little) as you want to your HSA, up to the maximum amount—which tends to increase every year and may be comparable to the amount of your deductible. (In 2009, the maximum was $5,950 for a family.) Once you hit a specific balance, your account may even offer investment options so that you have the opportunity to grow the money you're saving. And every dime you place in this account is also tax deductible.

You may pull from this account balance to pay for all medical expenses up to your deductible, and then pull from it for your percentage of costs beyond the deductible. You may use it to pay for co-pays, prescription drugs, and even some over-the-counter medications and the like. The list of qualified expenses grows every year and is available at the IRS Web site.

You can use money from the HSA to pay for braces, contacts, optometrist visits, and many types of health care expenses that may not even be covered under your health care plan. All tax-free. It's almost like siphoning your hard-earned dollars through an account that allows you to pay for nearly all normal health care expenses—things you pay for out of pocket anyway—only now it's tax-free.

The more you contribute to the account, the lower your income tax bill. For self-employed single parents, combine that savings with the deductibility of your premiums, and you pretty much end up paying no taxes on all your health care-related expenses. Yay.

Better yet, this is not a use it or lose it account like many employers offer (see FSAs). If you don't use all that you contribute to your HSA in one year, it rolls over to the next year. And the next.

And if you keep contributing every year, which is great way to lower your income tax bill, and you don't need all that money, you may use it free and clear once you retire (over age 65). Most accounts also offer investment options, and any interest you earn you may also withdraw tax-free (as long as it's for qualified medical expenses or you're over age 65).

An HSA is a tax haven for income. Paired with a high-deductible health care plan, it's a great way to keep your health care expenses down and save money on taxes at the same time. It's also another tax-advantaged way to save for retirement.

An HSA is also portable—it belongs to you, not your employer. If you leave your employer, all the money in the account stays with you. Even if you enroll in an HMO plan next, you may no longer contribute to the HSA but you can still access the money for qualified out-of-pocket medical expenses.

You may use it to pay for COBRA or other health care insurance premiums should you become unemployed. You can use it to pay for long-term care insurance premiums or long-term care expenses should you become disabled. Once you hit age 65, you can use it for anything. ·

Like a qualified retirement savings account, if you use the money for anything but qualified medical expenses (before age 65), you'll get hit with an extra 10 percent tax penalty. So don't use it for anything but health care expenses; with children on board that's usually not a problem.

Another beauty is that you do not *have* to contribute to the account, or can contribute whenever you want. Such as when you know you have health care expenses coming up—like a family visit to the dentist. Put money in a few weeks earlier; check to make sure the money is in your account. Then pay it out when you're at the dentist or when you get your bill.

Or, once you pay your bills, you can contribute to the account and then reimburse yourself with the expenses you paid. Many HSA providers provide checks and even debit cards that you can use like a VISA card at doctors' offices and pharmacies. Some even work at automatic teller machines so you can get cash. Keep all receipts and put them under "HSA Reimbursements" in your tax folder—staple reimbursement receipts to the bills they went toward.

If possible, try to use the debit card whenever you can, even to pay an invoice. The direct payout makes administrative tracking easier, plus you may get an ATM or per check charge if you use another method. All of these details will be included in your HSA information packet when you sign up—be sure you know all charges up front so you can utilize the least expensive method for this account.

Keep all of your medical bills and HSA reimbursement receipts. You don't have to submit these with your tax return but you will need them should you get audited.

Who can have an HSA? Any adult, so long as they meet the following criteria:

- Have coverage under an HSA-qualified "high-deductible health plan" (HDHP);
- Have no other medical coverage (like an employer-sponsored HMO);

- Are not enrolled in Medicare;
- Cannot be claimed as a dependent on someone else's tax return.

You can, however, have other forms of health insurance policies, such as specific-injury insurance or accident, disability, dental care, vision care, or long-term care insurance.

HEAD OF HOUSEHOLD TIP: ALTERNATE HEALTH CARE COVERAGE

Instead of paying out premiums for a dental or vision care policy, consider saving that discretionary income in an HSA and paying out only for expenses as needed. The HSA provides both tax advantages and you only pay for what you actually use, unlike an insurance policy.

Contributions to your HSA can be made by you, your employer, or both, up to a certain limit each year. You may deduct your contributions (even if you do not itemize deductions) when completing your federal income tax return.

The HSA is a very good reason to shop for alternate health care policies if your employer's plan seems too expensive. If your family is reasonably healthy, you can save money on premiums by securing a high-deductible plan, and set aside your savings through monthly installments in a HSA to pay for your out-of-pocket health care expenses.

Remember, if you decide to forgo employer-sponsored health care insurance, and you'll probably have to show evidence of alternate insurance if you do, be sure and ask for remuneration since your employer is saving money by not subsidizing your plan. You can use this money to help offset your monthly premiums or deposit it into your HSA.

Learning to evaluate health care insurance plans is a life skill. It's more important than straightening out your golf swing or learning to cook lasagna, so take the time you would normally devote to a less useful task and learn it.

For single parents, this is part of your financial education and a key to protecting your family. There isn't another adult in the family who's going to take over this task; it's all yours. Embrace it, and like all other drudgery, it will get easier each time you do it.

SIX

Housing

Housing as a single parent is one of those areas, like child care, where it's so much more difficult to provide for multiple people on a single income. If you receive child support, that's helpful, but divorce generally creates more housing expenses, not less.

Obviously, divorce splits a single household into two—with ensuing costs. In recent years, the concept of "bird nesting" has actually created a situation involving three households from a divorce.

In a nutshell, "nesting" is when a couple splits up, agrees to joint custody, and decides to let the children stay in the family home. Instead of shuffling them between two households, the children live in the house full-time and the parents take turns living in the house and shuffling to another locale on off days.

Obviously, this requires three separate housing expenses and usually works best as a temporary arrangement just after a separation. This arrangement requires ultimate collaboration between the estranged parents, and unless both have cheap alternate living arrangements (new love interest, parents, or friends), is probably reserved for people who can afford three different places to live.

Many times issues related to nesting, such as leaving dirty dishes in the sink and spending excess money from the housing budget, must be detailed in the separation agreement. On the other hand, such an arrangement does allow for the couple to maintain and grow equity in the home, which can be beneficial if the housing market is in a slump. Selling off the family home during a poor economic environment can have a devastating impact on long-term finances—for both spouses.

Many people believe that staying in the family home is less traumatic for the children of divorce. This is probably true, at least in the beginning. But remember that children are highly resilient beings. Even children who seem brittle as youngsters often emerge stronger as a result of adapting to a divorce situation.

It's tougher the older they get. In fact, nesting might be best employed when high-school age students are involved. A little more stability during this period—which is volatile regardless of parental issues—may be worth the effort, at least until they leave for college or are on their own.

Keep in mind, however, that divorce is hard on everyone. Children are generally not happy if their parents are unhappy. The best solution is to find an arrangement that works for both parents, and then make it work for the children. Initially, everyone is miserable. But children are not likely to move out of that arena until their primary role model finds a workable situation that alleviates unhappiness.

After enough time has passed to get everyone used to the idea that the marriage is over, do what you need to do to move on and get happy. Whether it's nesting, moving one parent out, or selling and moving everyone out, find the solution that works best both emotionally and financially. Your children will take their cue from your happiness.

Unless they're teenagers. There's nothing rational about being a teenager. Just know that angst and anxiety happens in even the most well-adjusted households, and don't kick yourself if your marriage fails during this volatile time for your children. Do what you need to do to get happy.

Teenagers will learn to get happy on their own terms, eventually. Divorce may not help, but it's hardly the only stimulus that causes teenage angst.

If you choose to nest, consider finding other nesters for the "alternate" households. Other separated or divorced couples may require alternate housing and can share expenses to help keep costs down.

When divorce became more mainstream during the 1970s, often men would share habitats until they figured out what to do next. One might buy a condominium and then have a rotation of separated and divorcing men funnel through, helping out with utilities and other expenses, on their way to the next chapter in their lives.

In the 1980s, *Kate & Allie* was a television show about divorced best friends who lived together in an apartment with their children after their respective divorces. This sort of arrangement not only helps out with expenses but gives both parents backup for child care, emergencies, and someone to talk to about raising children and other topics.

It seems less common now—having roommates with children. Much like today's resistance to carpooling, people like their independence and are used to having a home of their own. It's tough to imagine sharing space with outsiders once you've lived as a closed-knit family.

But cohabiting does solve for a lot of financial issues, and if you set up an arrangement as temporary, it may be an ideal solution. Particularly if both parties establish set goals based on the arrangement, such as saving a certain amount of money for a down payment on a house or getting out of debt.

If you own a home and are struggling to make ends meet, consider sharing your space and expenses with another single parent. If you don't yet have a home of your own but need a secure, loving environment to house your family, consider approaching another single parent with a temporary arrangement.

RENTING

You've heard it before: Renting is like throwing money out of the window. That's a financial mentality, but the fact is that renting is a way of life for many single parents.

There are several factors to consider when renting—and the first is not money. It's safety. Your first priority is not to live somewhere cheap; it's to live somewhere safe.

If you can live somewhere safe, that's cheap; *Yay*. If not, live somewhere safe until you find somewhere both safe and cheap.

Trade up when you can, but don't go overboard. It's important for children to live a lifestyle reasonably comparable to their peer group. However, if divorce drops your standard of living substantially, don't feel you have to drive yourself deep into debt to keep up with your friends' lifestyles.

HEAD OF HOUSEHOLD TIP: VALUES-BASED BUYING

Every decision you make needs to reflect your standard of living. If you're fortunate to stay in your current household, start making value decisions about the things you used to buy but can no longer afford. Brand name clothes can be purchased at discount stores just as easily as department stores. Make meaningful but fewer purchases, and recognize that your 13-year-old will not suffer if she has to make do with $40 jeans instead of $150 jeans.

Make money decisions that make sense. If you insist on a certain quality or brand name, then simply do not buy as often as you used to. If you're willing to shop at lower-priced stores like Target or Wal-Mart, give your children more flexibility in their choices so it seems like a treat.

It's always best not to start off life as a snob, and then you don't have to lower your standards. But if you approach all of your purchases going forward—whether you make $20,000 or $200,000 a year—with a practical, values-based approach, you'll find you can adjust your mind to meet whatever standard you can afford.

Ask yourself these two questions every time you're considering a purchase:

1. Do I *need* this?
2. Can I *live without* this?

Don't even ask yourself if you can afford something; just assume you can't. Then these two questions take on more meaning, because they reflect your values, not your taste.

The "Can I live without this" question usually gets answered in the affirmative when you've either wanted something a long time and now you feel like you can afford it, or when you really need to pamper yourself and the purchase is a low-cost way to fulfill that need.

If you're looking at a $300 pair of shoes when you ask these questions, you won't even have to get to the second question. Be honest.

When you get a new job or decent increase in salary, you may want to trade up where you live. Consider the following questions:

1. Is your current home safe? Affordable?
2. Can you get the same value for the same (or slightly more) money somewhere that you would like better?
3. Are you comfortable where you live now; do you or your children really want to move?
4. Is your current home in a good school district?
5. Can you afford to move to an area in a good school district?

6. Is this the best time to move? Would it be better to reconsider in another six months or a year?

7. Are you happy where you currently live? Miserable?

8. Does your child care where you live right now (when they're preschool age, probably not; the older they get, the more they care)?

9. Are you currently near your work or child care provider? Consider that low commute times and predictable traffic are crucial for single parents.

By the time your children reach school age, you may want to work your way into the school district of your choice. Unless you can afford and want to send your children to a private school, let the choice of good schools be your guide on where to live.

If that seems limiting, consider the alternative. You could be married and have to make this decision based on the needs and wants of you, your children *and* your spouse and perhaps your spouse's job. As a single person, you need to consider only yourself and your children. This is one of the benefits of being a single parent. Given the alternative, the school district limitation may not seem so limiting after all.

If you find a safe, cheap place to live near grandma, or your affluent sister and her family, in a good school district, and you're happy living there until you're a ripe old age, *yay*. If not, keep looking. Remember, the younger the children are, the better they adapt. Keep looking while they are young; find a place and stick where you are by the time they get older.

RENTING VERSUS BUYING

There are valid arguments that support renting over owning a home, and they are particularly popular right now due to the housing bubble and poor economic environment. Buying versus renting is usually about timing—what you can currently afford to do and what is the current environment in the real estate market and mortgage industry.

In general, the case for renting over buying can be divided into two categories: (1) Saving/investing and (2) Lifestyle. The saving/investing argument typically assumes that a renter will pay a lower monthly payment for housing than a homeowner, which is not universally true. Many people who buy a home do so because, especially with the size of a home necessary to raise children, their monthly outlay is about the same as renting. But if you do pay significantly less in rent than for a mortgage, the financial argument for renting assumes that you will diligently invest this substantial savings for a higher long-term return than an investment in real estate has historically yielded. Does that sound like you?

In the real world of single parenting in which I live, that describes a very small, almost minuscule percentage of the population. I can think of one single mom who fits that description. And the only reason she's still renting is so that when she remarries she can combine her savings with her husband's (whom she has yet to meet) in order to buy a big house together.

The second argument in the case for renting is about lifestyle. Granted, if you are a minimalist when it comes to home furnishings and would prefer to spend your time and money on travel and out-of-the-home activities rather than puttering around on a Sunday afternoon raking the yard or fixing a leak under the kitchen sink, you've got me there. Rent away.

I do still long for the days when I called my property manager to replace a burned-out lightbulb in my rental loft's track lighting. But now, I rather enjoy my honed skills with my trusty flathead and Phillips screwdrivers. In fact, home owning has also helped me become a better-rounded single parent. You see, my technical proficiency (or lack thereof) has also served to expose my sons to those enviable masculine skills they might never have had to learn living in a rental. Plus, I make them take out the infiltrated mice traps to the trash (now that's manly).

Despite having to pay taxes, insurance, and maintenance, given the fact that the vast majority of people sell their houses for more than they paid for them, the balance sheet usually tips in favor of home owning instead of home renting. It also helps my children feel more secure and on par with the majority of their peers, and that's worth far more to me than financial gain.

BUYING

Value means something different to different people. For some, buying a huge house in a mediocre school district means living large. However, they're trading values. Either they're not placing a high value on their child's education and trading it for a specific house, or they place an equal value on education and perhaps decide to put their child in a private school.

Some people can afford to do both. But for others, this is how a lot of people start the cycle of living beyond their means. They want it all. This is a luxury single parents can ill afford.

WHERE TO BUY

If you're flexible about in which part of the country you could live, keep in mind that places you may consider less desirable may also be the least expensive, with good schools and health care systems. These might be places in the Midwest like Michigan, Illinois, and Iowa. Many companies have moved their corporate headquarters to small cities in states like these to help cut costs, so jobs are abundant.

If you work a public service job like schoolteacher or fireman, your earning potential as a general rule may be limited. Living in a town where housing is affordable, commutes are short, and other expenses remain low can help maximize the money you earn and provide a higher standard of living than that of a larger, more expensive city.

Do your research. Look for places with low unemployment, low-cost living, and highly ranked schools. As a general rule, they tend to exist in family-oriented communities, not resort towns.

DEMYSTIFYING THE HOME BUYING PROCESS

Buying a home for the first time can be a scary prospect. But like every other large-scale undertaking, the more you know, the easier the process and the more confidence you gain. It also helps to break down the process into bite-sized steps.

Know Thy Credit Report

One of the ten commandments of home buying is to know and understand what's on your credit report. It can take a long time to clear up problems on a credit report, so if you're considering buying a home, be sure to get a copy of your report three to six months before starting the process.

Research Online

The Internet makes it easier to compare rates, options, and fees when shopping for a mortgage loan, not to mention that the application process can be faster and easier.

Online you may use electronic tools to find out which type of loan works best for your situation, how much you qualify for, and various payment schedules for loan amounts. Since the Internet process removes the tension of high-pressure sales, it's much easier to shop via the Internet than to pick up the phone or visit a mortgage broker face-to-face.

However, if this is your first time buying a home and you have a lot of questions, you may want to combine some basic information research online and then schedule an in-person interview with a mortgage broker. Go to the meeting armed with your questions—that's what the initial research is for.

It's best to read and be a little prepared. If you think you'll learn everything you need to know in a one-hour meeting, what you'll eventually learn is that you don't know what you don't know—so you don't know all the right questions to ask.

The more you research, the more you'll learn, and the more questions will crop up that lead you to a far more productive discussion with a broker than if you expect a Mortgage 101 class in your first meeting.

Applying for a mortgage and buying a house is a complicated process, so learn as much as you can on your own so you're not at the mercy of one professional's opinion and experiences (or the lack of them).

Whether you're interested in using the World Wide Web for the entire home buying process or just for one aspect such as loan shopping, the following sites can help make the chore a little more convenient:

- www.realtor.com—view most home listings throughout the United States; a good place to start to get an idea of what type of house you can get for the price.

- www.homefair.com—an online resource for all things—home buying, renting, and moving—but a particularly good source to look up the strongest ranked schools in the area you're seeking. Once you find a few schools you like, narrow your home search to those areas to find out the range of housing prices in that school district.

- www.ashi.com—the American Society of Home Inspectors, to help you find a local inspector for the new home you hope to buy. A real estate agent should also have references for local inspectors, mortgage brokers, etc.

- www.lendingtree.com and www.eloan.com—just a couple of the plethora of Web sites that allow you to compare mortgage loans.

Buying a Home (Away from Home)

In 1998, I was living in Los Angeles and decided to buy a house and move back to the South before my son started a new school year. I researched as much as possible online—including cities, schools, and homes in the areas I was considering. Once I narrowed down a region,

I contacted a few real estate agents and finally went with one with whom I established a rapport via phone and e-mail. She profiled my wish list and sent me listings of homes for sale in that area. My son and I made a visit during his Spring Break and ended up putting a contract on a house by the end of the week.

My agent procured a local mortgage broker, who happened to be her ex-husband, and I witnessed firsthand how she tore him to shreds in order to get me the lowest interest rate possible at the time. We were able to conduct all escrow-related business by phone, fax, and e-mail; my agent handled the inspection, walk-through, and I granted her limited power of attorney to take my place at closing.

This was my first home-buying experience, made unbelievably easier thanks to the Internet and the tireless buyer's agent who looked after us like we were family. Best of all, my son and I sent our worldly possessions off in a moving van and took a two-week cross-country camping trip en route to our new home in Virginia. We weathered campsite visits from both a skunk and a mountain lion in the Redwood Forest, tracked bear and moose (by car) in Yellowstone, and took photos of my son under every "Welcome To" state sign we ventured past. The only glitch was arriving at our new home on an early Sunday evening to discover the house key was not left for us.

Alas, it was a fortuitous way to meet our new neighbors.

Beware the Low Down Payment

The mortgage loan industry has experienced widespread trends from the low-interest rate environment of the 1990s to the subprime mess, credit crunch, and housing crisis further into the new millennium. For years, low and no down payment mortgage loans were prevalent. We have learned, however, that while getting into a home with 2–5 percent down is a dream come true for many Americans, the low-down-payment mortgage leads to several drawbacks. These include

- Monthly mortgage payments are higher because you've borrowed so much money;
- Home loans over a certain amount generally offer higher interest rates;
- Most lenders require you to carry private mortgage insurance (PMI) until you have at least 20 percent equity in your home;
- An adjustable (variable) rate mortgage can be a killer when rates rise.

In short, your monthly payment will be higher, you'll pay much more in interest, and you'll pay an additional amount in PMI on top of your loan.

For a single parent in particular, with a precarious single income, a fixed rate mortgage is generally the way to go. A roof over your head with no surprises, year in and year out.

CONTROL WHAT YOU CAN CONTROL

The economy moves in cycles—nothing ever stays the same. There's inflation, deflation, low interest rates, high interest rates, low unemployment rates followed by rampant layoffs—these are factors you personally are never going to be able to control.

What you can control, to a great extent, are your own expenses. Don't buy more house than you can afford. Don't stretch your finances because you "fell in love" with a particular home. If divorce and remarriage rates have taught us nothing else, they have taught us that it is possible, indeed, to "fall in love" again.

Be smart, smart, smart. If you can't afford the asking price for the house of your dreams, make a lower offer. You never know. Be prepared to walk away and find the real home of your dreams. You can dream new dreams just as well as the old ones.

By keeping your housing expenses as low and affordable as possible, you put yourself in the best position possible if and when—most likely when—the bad stuff happens. You lose your job. Oil prices skyrocket. The cost of groceries goes through the roof.

There are ways to backtrack and "do over" your mortgage decision, but it's a lot easier to get it right the first time. In short, work toward making at least a 20 percent down payment and get a fixed low-interest rate loan.

Private Mortgage Insurance

Your lender will likely require you to pay PMI as part of your monthly mortgage payment if you put down less than 20 percent for your home. This may run anywhere from $50 to $200 each month. The amount is based on how much you owe on the mortgage. The lender isn't required to drop your PMI until you accumulate or pay off up to 22 percent of the house's original purchase price.

It's not all bad. The good news is that you can request to stop paying PMI once the equity you own in your home reaches 20 percent—which can happen due to any upgrades you make, rising prices in the housing market, etc.

It's not unusual for home equity to reach this point before you actually pay up to that amount due to inherent increases in the housing market.

To drop PMI once you reach 20 percent equity, you will need to initiate the request to cancel PMI, and you'll probably have to pay for a home assessment to verify what your home is worth (cost $150 and up).

By law, lenders must cancel PMI on their end once you own 22 percent equity in the home. You can save yourself a decent amount of money ($1,000–2,000 in a year) by initiating cancellation at 20 percent. You can keep up with the calculation yourself or periodically ask your lender if you've reached 20 percent equity yet.

Currently, you may deduct the PMI you pay on your tax return if you originate(d) your mortgage anytime in the years 2007 through 2010 (but not if you're paying on an older loan). Whether the PMI deduction will continue after 2010 is anyone's guess.

IF YOU MUST PUT DOWN LESS THAN 20 PERCENT . . .

As stated in the beginning of this book, it may simply take longer when you're a single parent to afford the things you want. It may take 10 years to save a 10 percent down payment for a house. Based on that savings rate, it could take another 10 to come up with 20 percent, which of course would be even more money because housing prices would rise in that time frame.

Buying a house isn't too unlike having children in that . . . there's never really a "right" time. You're never really fully prepared for the responsibility you're about to take on. Take a deep breath. Sometimes you just have to make a decision, and then make it work.

So if you're ready to own your own home, there are alternate ways to drum up that 20 percent down payment.

One way is to apply for a "piggyback mortgage," combining your first mortgage with a home equity loan. Here's an example of how a piggyback works. Say you want to purchase a home for $200,000. You put down 10 percent, or $20,000. You borrow $150,000 on your first mortgage. Then, at the same time, you take out a home equity loan to the tune of $30,000.

Right off the bat, you may deduct the interest you pay on your tax return for *both* the first mortgage and the home equity loan. You also avoid PMI payments altogether.

The rate you receive on the piggybacked home equity loan will likely be higher than that on your first mortgage, depending on your creditworthiness. However, because you've used the home equity loan to reduce the amount borrowed on the primary mortgage, you'll lower your monthly payments on your first mortgage.

Keep in mind, though, that you'll be making essentially two mortgage payments. If you get into a situation where you can't make one or the other payment, your home is at risk. Do the research and the math to determine for yourself if it is wiser to take out two loans or just pay the PMI until you reach 20 percent equity—which may happen long before you pay off the equity loan.

HOW TO QUALIFY FOR A MORTGAGE LOAN

The good news about relaxed lending standards over the last 20 years is that it is now commonplace for single people—women in particular—to qualify for a mortgage loan. This was not always the case, so acknowledge and appreciate that you now enjoy a privilege largely unavailable to your parents' generation.

There are two factors that matter most in qualifying for a mortgage:

1. How timely you've paid your bills in the past, and
2. Whether the house you want to buy is worth the purchase price.

The following steps will help ease the process of qualifying for your first home loan:

Start hoarding money each month for a down payment. You may want to open a separate savings account just for this purpose—preferably at a credit union as interest rates are frequently higher. Stay focused on your goal and stash any windfalls to this account, such as a work bonus or tax refund.

Don't stop saving just because you think you have enough for a down payment. Plan for a cash cushion beyond your down payment; lenders don't want to see you go broke by buying a house (neither do you).

The first step in the home buying process is to get prequalified or—better yet—preapproved for a mortgage, as this gives you a price range in which to shop and increases your chances of having an offer accepted.

You can enlist the aid of a mortgage broker to shop for the best interest rates and least stringent qualifying requirements. If you have lots of questions and prefer hand-holding, meet with several brokers face-to-face and go with the one who satisfactorily answers your questions and is willing to give you lots of time, information, and advice so you feel comfortable and secure moving forward.

If you prefer to do your own research and take a more independent approach, there are a plethora of Internet resources for both learning about the mortgage and home buying process, and actually applying for loans online.

Collect the documents you'll need for the qualifying process. These may include

- Two to three years of tax returns;
- Two to three years of W-2 forms;
- A recent paycheck stub that includes your Social Security number;
- Investment records and bank statements;
- Statements documenting other sources of income, including a second job, overtime, commissions and bonuses, interest and dividend income, Social Security payments, alimony, and child support;
- A complete list of creditors, your minimum monthly payments, and total balances;
- Canceled checks for current rent payments.

HOUSE SHOPPING

Once you are prequalified for a mortgage, you can shop for homes within this price range. Nearly all homes are listed with a multiple listing service (MLS) number. This is mostly true with houses listed with a real estate agency, but many homes for sale by owner have the option to get an MLS number assigned now as well.

You can search for MLS listings online to help narrow your search. Try a mass national listing such as www.realtor.com for the most comprehensive database. From there you can find links to local real estate agencies that represent the homeowners listed and can also offer you a buyer's agent as well.

A buyer's agent is a licensed real estate agent whose sole mission is to represent the home buyer's interests, both in matching the right house to your needs and at the right price. Real estate agents typically have a wide network of mortgage brokers, lenders, home inspectors, and real estate attorneys to help you in the home buying process.

A buyer's agent is paid by the home seller. Both the seller's agent and the buyer's agent are paid a commission based on the home's sale price.

When you see a "For Sale By Owner" (FSBO) sign, the price may or may not be lower than other homes in the area. Some homeowners use the fact that they don't have to pay agent commissions as an advantage to offer the home at a lower price. Others may offer the home at the same market price so they can pocket the extra money themselves.

Keep in mind that real estate agents do not like FSBO homeowners, as they often will not receive a commission for the sale and believe the FSBO sellers do not follow the same "code of ethics" of the real estate agent industry.

If you fall in love with a house being sold by the owner, be prepared to either negotiate your agent's commission as part of the sale and paid by the home seller, or pay your buyer's agent directly out of your own pocket. Agents typically work exclusively on commission, so they need to be compensated for the time they spend helping you find a home, and work with you to find a mortgage broker, conduct an inspection, and close the sale.

A buyer's agent can do a comparative market analysis (CMA) of any home in which you're interested to see if it is worth the price offered. This is a detailed listing of similar homes in the area that have recently sold or are listed for sale. He or she can also advise you on whether you can and/ or should offer a lower price given the current market.

Whether or not you wish to use a buyer's agent is strictly a personal choice, but it is a very common practice in today's real estate market. Particularly for time-strapped single parents, this type of representation may be your best choice—especially considering you don't have to pay their fee.

Be wary of a buyer's agent who tries to sell you a home in which he is also listed as the seller's agent. In this situation, the agent will receive a double commission—as both the homeowner's and the buyer's representative. It's supposed to be the agent's job to represent the sole interest of his client, but in this case he has two clients so it's seemingly impossible to represent both sides of the coin adequately. An agent who offers to put himself in this position is frequently most interested in his own best interest.

HOME EQUITY

Once you've bought a home, you may immediately or eventually have home equity. In other words, your purchase equals wealth. Your equity may be the down payment you laid out for the purchase, or you may have gotten a deal whereas the home you purchased was actually worth more in the market than the price you paid.

Either way, if you need to pay for college, a home improvement, a car, or consolidate debt, the equity in your home could be your ticket to cash. Tread carefully here, but you should know your options.

Studies have shown that, on average, the younger you buy a house, the wealthier you will be in your lifetime. One of the greatest components of wealth in the United States is home equity. It can be used as collateral for a cash loan—known as a home equity loan.

Home equity loans or lines of credit are usually the lowest rate loans you can get when compared to unsecured loans or car loans. The most important qualification is that you have equity in your home, so usually this is someone who has either paid a large down payment on his or her house or owned it for a number of years.

There are two types of equity loans: term or closed-end loans—also known as a second mortgage—and lines of credit. Closed-end loans are generally available with fixed interest rates and allow homeowners to borrow a set amount of money for a fixed period of time, typically 10–15 years. Historically, fixed interest rates on home equity loans have run higher than that of a first mortgage but significantly lower than that for a credit card or personal loan. With a good credit score and significant equity in your home, you can qualify for a good, competitive rate.

A home equity line of credit (HELOC), on the other hand, offers a variable interest rate and works with a revolving line of credit, kind of like a big credit card. You pay a variable interest rate and have a minimum payment due each month based on how much of the credit line you've used. You can draw on your line of credit whenever you want. Your interest rate will depend on your credit score and is subject to change based on the current interest rate environment.

Remember that interest rates are cyclical, so over a long time period such as the one in which you may pay back a home equity loan, rates are likely to swing both high and low. If you need a small amount of money, current interest rates are low, and you expect to pay off any borrowed amount in less than a year's time, maintaining a HELOC may be a good option.

However, if you need to borrow a large sum and it will take years to pay back, then it's likely that your best option is to procure a low fixed rate for a home equity loan. Again, a roof over your head with no surprises, year in and year out.

With both a home equity loan and a HELOC, the interest you pay on the loan may be tax deductible, just like on your mortgage.

The typical home equity loan or line of credit uses the equity you already own in your home as collateral, known as the loan-to-value (LTV) ratio, for a home mortgage. However, you may also qualify for a 125 percent LTV loan in which you may borrow 25 percent more than your home is worth.

Referred to as no-equity loans, these hybrid loans have combined components of home equity and an unsecured personal loan. Unsecured loans typically call for a higher interest rate and do not allow you to utilize the mortgage interest tax deduction on interest charged on the portion of the loan that exceeds your home's value.

For obvious reasons, this type of loan is not a good idea. It's bad enough to pay for something you can't afford to pay in cash. But when you borrow more money against your home than your home is actually worth, you put yourself and your family at risk ... of being homeless. And still owing money even after you've lost your home.

HEAD OF HOUSEHOLD TIP: USING HOME EQUITY FOR COLLEGE EXPENSES

If you're fretting about how to pay for your child's college education, home equity is definitely an option. But first you should complete your student's Free Application for Federal Student Aid (FAFSA), the form used by the U.S. Department of Education to determine your Expected Family Contribution (EFC). This determination is made based on a "needs analysis" of your financial information, such as income, assets, and other household information, as completed on the FAFSA form.

Here's the tip. If you apply for a HELOC or HEL and transfer this money into one of your bank accounts, you must report this cash on your FAFSA form. Such an influx of cash in your account will likely increase your EFC, which means your student will qualify for less financial aid.

Wait until you receive the results of your financial aid application before applying or receiving home equity cash. If you don't have enough to cover the cost of the EFC, then consider the home equity route. Also, weigh the advantages of using home equity versus student loans, which are also offered at relatively low interest rates, and do not put your home at risk.

If you do use cash from your home equity, pull out only what you need each year. Remember that tons of home equity cash sitting in your bank account will make you appear far more wealthy than you probably are, and hurt your student's chances for financial aid.

HOW TO QUALIFY FOR A HOME EQUITY LOAN

You may apply for a home equity loan with the same lender that carries your first mortgage, but it isn't necessary. Most banks and credit unions offer home equity loans, and there are currently a large number of Web-based brokers who will help shop your loan application for the best rates.

You typically need to own about 20 percent equity in your home to get a lending institution's lowest rates. Normally, the underwriting requirements are much less stringent than when applying for a first mortgage.

To qualify, your lender will consider your credit score, debt-to-income ratio, regular income, and the amount of equity in your home based on a current appraisal. Loan administration and appraisal fees may be waived or negotiated down.

Although home equity loans offer many benefits, they also involve some risk. Be cautioned that when you choose to borrow against the equity of your home, you must absolutely be fiscally responsible. Any time a home is used as collateral, you run the risk of losing it if you fail to make the loan payments—just like your first mortgage.

This is a particularly precarious situation for a single parent with only one income. Should you lose that income, you could lose your home. Not necessarily because you can't make the mortgage, but because you can't also pay the second mortgage.

Other loan alternatives do not have the option to take your house, so give it serious consideration before using your home equity. It is not to be used to fund your vacations or other superfluous expenses.

In fact, it's best to consider your home equity as your emergency safety net.

HEAD OF HOUSEHOLD TIP: APPLY WHILE GAINFULLY EMPLOYED

While home equity may make a good safety net, you may not be able to tap it if you lose your job or some other calamity prevails upon your life. The best time to apply for a home equity loan is when you don't need it: When you're gainfully employed, with low debt, and have sufficient funds in your bank accounts.

For this reason, it's best to apply for a HELOC instead of a loan. With a line of credit, the money is available if you need it, but you don't have to make payments with interest on money you haven't borrowed yet. With a loan, you start paying out interest on money you don't need, and that's not smart.

You can always convert a line of credit to a home equity loan once you borrow money. This will help you secure a fixed interest rate and predictable expense.

Not many banks will take a chance on an unemployed single parent homeowner, so don't wait until you're in dire circumstances to qualify.

HOMEOWNER TAX DEDUCTIONS

The money you pay in interest on your mortgage—and typically on a home equity loan or line of credit secured by your home—may be deducted on your tax return. And since you get to deduct the interest you pay on the mortgage, home ownership actually helps reduce the taxes you pay on your work income. For this reason alone, owning is better than renting. Yay.

With renting, not only do you never see a return on your monthly rent in terms of wealth-building equity, but you don't get to deduct the rent you pay from your taxes. That's why they say it's like throwing money out of the window. Actually, it's like living in a hotel indefinitely.

SEVEN

Income

Some people were born to work. Work is their challenge, their fulfillment; it defines them. For others, work is a means to an end. You can live to work, or you can work to live. The choice is different for everyone, and of course, there are plenty of folks who fall somewhere in between.

A single parent has two full-time jobs: The one she gets paid for, and the one she pays out for.

Oh sure, two-income parents may have to work and parent also, but that's more like three full-time jobs split between two people. It's a partnership, with flextime, when they can negotiate who does what, when, and serve as backup for each other.

The single parent lifestyle is a little bit different. Not only do you carry the burden of bringing home the bacon *and* frying it up in the pan, but the stress of having no other choice, having no long-term backup plan, and knowing that failure is not an option is an extra weight you carry on your shoulders every day—24/7, 365 days a year.

And you feel it, quite literally, like a 10-pound weight sitting squarely across your shoulders.

Fortunately, you get used to it. Like it does for everyone else, stress weighs more on some days than others. And like having your child around, you can't imagine not having it. In some ways, it's a motivator. For most single parents, financial security is the greatest challenge—and the ultimate carrot.

So if you're lucky, you find a way to earn income doing something that you enjoy. And if not, you just find a way to earn income.

JOB VERSUS CAREER

Many people, like doctors, lawyers, teachers, and firemen, choose a profession and stay with it their whole lives. That's a career. Others, like waiters, retail clerks, and many college business majors, get out and get a job. Then another. And then another, and so on. Sometimes it works out to a career, other times it's just a series of jobs.

Neither route really matters. All that matters is that you pursue work you enjoy and that you learn to manage however much money you make.

Because somewhere along the way you may get laid off, fired, or quit because your boss is an idiot and all the while you wish you could just work a low-stress, undemanding little job on some tropical island (with a good public school system).

The thing about money is that it's only money. It's a means to an end. Unless you're very unusual, you don't actually want a bunch of green, rectangular pieces of paper parked out in your driveway or propped up on the fireplace mantel. You want the things money can buy you. You probably hardly ever even use money anymore, what, with the advent of credit and debit cards and the magic of the Internet where all you need to buy things is a keyboard.

So while money is necessary to provide for the things you and your family need and want, what should be more important is what you do to earn it. Again, this is where your values and the values you teach your children come into play.

If you hate your job, there's no hiding that from your children. Whether you complain incessantly or never speak ill of work, they intuitively know; even if they don't know they know.

That's because your child knows every line in your face. She knows the things that make you laugh and what sets off your temper. Children are good at this. They are experts at pushing your buttons, so they are very tuned in to your moods and know when someone else has been pushing your buttons.

If you're going to spend approximately 40 hours (or more) away from the full-time job of raising your child every week, then you need to enjoy what you're doing during that time.

Everyone goes through bad patches in a job, just like in a relationship. And just like in a relationship, there comes a time where you need to decide whether to commit yourself to making that job work and finding a way to be happy with it, or move on and find something (or someone) new.

Many single parents have already faced this situation through a divorce, and it was probably a lot tougher than deciding to leave a job. This makes single parents particularly experienced and well-qualified at making this type of decision.

Use your experience to your advantage. Make a decision, and then make it work.

Your happiness and job satisfaction affects your parenting. It affects your finances and income-earning ability. It affects your physical and mental health. And it has a serious and long-term impact on the values you teach your children.

Do you want to teach them to find a way to earn income doing something that they enjoy or to just find a way to earn income?

SELF-EMPLOYMENT

There are tons of ways to make money, as evidenced on late night television. Perhaps you need to hold a regular steady job but are looking for a way to earn extra income. The rest of this chapter is devoted to some of the options you may wish to consider.

HOME-BASED BUSINESS

Thinking about starting up your own home-based business? According to the U.S. Small Business Administration (SBA), more than half of all U.S. businesses are based out of an owner's home. In fact, Apple Computer, Ford Motor Company, Hershey Chocolate, and Mary Kay Cosmetics all started out as home-based businesses.

For many, running a Small Office/Home Office ("SOHO") business out of the home is an ideal job, but doing so requires a certain degree of financial stability and discipline. It's also a big departure from the regular paycheck and benefits of an employer. The following are some of the more practical issues you should consider before taking the leap to entrepreneur.

ENTREPRENEURSHIP

Budding writers are often told by educators and mentors to "write what you know." The same can be held true for starting your own in-home business.

If you have a lot of experience working in one industry or business discipline, that's a good place to start in terms of opening up a business from your home. Even if you don't have years of experience in the business of your choice—say you're an office worker who wants to become a stay-at-home mom and open an in-home day care center—you still have a great chance of success as long as you pursue an interest or hobby about which you feel passionate and dedicated.

The following are the most popular venues for turning your full-time job into a home-based career:

- As a natural outgrowth of what you're doing in a corporate environment, many SOHO owners become consultants to their network of contacts, even to their former employers who can vouch for their experience and training.
- Many home-based ventures stem from a hobby or avocation that creates enough demand to earn a living, such as gardening, carpentry, or catering.
- Internet empowerment—it has become easy for many people to start up an online business, even with no prior experience, such as a niche retail distributor.

PREPARE YOURSELF FINANCIALLY

There are drawbacks to starting your own business. If you leave a full-time job and start cold turkey, you may have start-up costs and have to adjust to a lower income. Revenues in the first year or two may be spotty until you develop a network of customers. And if you have a particularly time- or labor-intensive business, your potential income is limited unless you hire and train others to help you, which means a further investment in overhead.

With this in mind, the following are ways to help secure your current financial picture before you launch your own small business:

- Save up a year's worth of income as your financial cushion;
- Get your credit card debt under control first;
- If home shopping, get approved for a mortgage before you quit your full-time job;
- You may also want to apply for a HELOC in case you get strapped for cash later on;
- Investigate health insurance alternatives before you quit your job.

SMALL BUSINESS LOANS

Unless you have wealthy benefactors and silent partners, nearly every small business goes looking for a loan at one point or another. Usually commercial loans are sought once the business is a few years old and somewhat on its feet, as loan requirements can be quite stringent and you must prove your ability to repay the loan.

A small business owner seeking a loan must have a very specific plan in mind for how he will spend the money. In fact, it can't just be in his mind; his goals must be written down in the form of a well-documented business plan. Some of the acceptable reasons for seeking a loan include

- To renovate or expand the current business premises;
- To finance equipment or machinery;
- To boost working capital;
- To purchase land or buildings;
- To construct commercial buildings;
- To refinance debt or seasonal lines of credit.

LOAN RESOURCES

The most logical first step to loan hunting is to try a local bank. You'll have better luck and a more understanding relationship if you work with a local entity that is already familiar with your business and its place within your community. If you have your personal and/or business checking and savings accounts with the bank, that's all the more advantageous.

The second place to look is to the SBA, which offers a loan guarantee program with less stringent requirements than many lending institutions. Other places to seek small business loans include commercial finance companies, venture capital firms, local economic development companies, and equipment leasing vendors.

You're in good company when you take the SBA route, as such renowned companies as Federal Express, Intel, Nike, Apple, AOL, and Ben & Jerry's started out using the SBA loan guarantee program.

THE LOAN PROCESS

If you apply for a loan under the SBA program, you will have to complete your end of the paperwork. This includes providing the following:

- Personal financial statements for the past three years;
- Business and/or personal tax returns;
- Monthly cash flow projections;

- A detailed business plan;
- Profiles of the experience of your company's top management;
- Company financial statements, including balance sheet and income statement.

Most importantly, you must show how you will use the loan, how much you need to borrow, and how you plan to repay the loan. If you wish to apply for a loan with a bank or other traditional lender, ask for referrals from other businesses at or near your location, or find out what banks your competitors use. It's always best to go with a lender who understands your business.

HOME-BASED BUSINESS: ARE YOU GOOD ALONE?

A home-based business is not for everyone. Some people just can't take the long hours of peace and quiet with no interaction among coworkers. This is something you may want to seriously consider before you decide to commit to a home-based business: How well do you spend time alone?

To help counteract the isolation of working by yourself all day long, join professional business groups, plan weekly lunches with colleagues or other home workers, and network with people inside and outside your profession. Consider renting space in an office environment with other entrepreneurs to share resources, expenses, and a more lively, convivial work environment.

SET YOUR WORK HOURS

If you do find you're suited to working alone, one of the great advantages to working from home is setting your own work hours. If you're a morning person, work in the morning. If you're a night owl, after midnight can provide the quietest time to concentrate. Plus, you may have the flexibility to quit in the middle of the day to accommodate carpooling, doctor's visits, ball games, and whatever else interrupts your workday.

While that may sound great, one of the problems with working a home-based business is that you can, and will be tempted to, work all the time. Since you never know how steady your work will be, it's tough to turn down jobs. Consequently, you'll likely find yourself working in snatches whenever you have free time, including nights, weekends, and vacations.

One of the biggest problems that comes with a home-based business is working too many hours—not too few. As long as you are enjoying the work, this is not your worst problem. But as a single parent, you have another full-time job to which you must attend. So stay tuned in to the fact that this can be a problem.

As much as possible, try to structure your work hours to accommodate both your family's needs and your best hours of concentration. Work to locate your home office geographically away from the center of the family universe, where the most noise will disturb you. Imagine that if you have to work while your children are about, then it will take much longer to concentrate and get the job done if you are constantly distracted.

Lay down strict rules about why and when you may be disturbed, and make sure everyone understands that this is a job—it pays for television, video games, new clothes, and whatever else matters to them. Make it clear that your children and their visiting friends are to respect your work environment in the same way they would if they had to interrupt you at an employer's office.

WHAT TO DO?

Your best chance of success is to focus all of your energy and resources on a business idea that is the most viable and suits your abilities, expertise, and lifestyle as a single parent.

One way to help you evaluate your idea is to draw a matrix of your interests and skills. Across the top of a piece of paper, write down your business venture ideas. Down the left side of the paper, list your skills, areas of expertise, educational background, experience, as well as your interests and personality traits. Then place a check mark under the business ideas that can best utilize those individual personal qualities.

Once you've completed the exercise matching each business idea with each personal quality, you may see one business venture emerge as a clear-cut winner or at least narrow down your choices. Now draw up a list of challenges and requirements this business must be flexible enough to accommodate with your other (non-income producing) full-time job—that of single parent.

For example, if you've got to be free for your child's soccer games on Sunday afternoons, a residential real estate buyer's agent (and requisite Sunday open houses) may not be your thing. Consider what you want to accomplish and what you're willing to compromise or give up to accomplish your income-earning goals.

Remember why you want the additional income. If it's because you are seeking a better quality of life, does that include missing your child's soccer games?

Pursue What You Do Well—and Enjoy

I write. I always have, with early efforts including my second-grade story "Candy Land" (based on the board game) with chocolate rivers and peppermint trees, to my sixth-grade masterpiece, "Here, Piggy Piggy"—a candid retelling of my mother trying to protect me from an escaped wild boar that ran into my backyard when I was five. Trapped between the house and me hanging from the monkey bars, at first my mother coaxed the 500-pound animal toward her with "Here, Piggy Piggy." (My cat came running.) Then, when two policemen rounded the yard from both sides with guns drawn, she yelled out maniacally, "You're going to shoot each other!" It's a shame this exciting true-life tale never found its way to the cinema. But I digress.

Because I have always been a writer, at least in some capacity through-out my corporate career, making the transition to a freelance writer was quite easy. I converted what I did best and enjoyed the most in my work into a full-time consulting capacity. Even as I worked a couple of full-time jobs intermittently throughout my freelance career, I kept my cache of clients and pitched articles to publications on a part-time basis. This allowed me to maintain my home office tax deduction as well as various expenses, including my computer.

MARKET RESEARCH

Whatever it is you want to do, chances are you will have to sell it to others. So you need to know who your market is. Determine who out there is interested in buying what you have to offer, whether you're a massage therapist or a roofer.

One of the first things you want to do before jumping into a new business is conduct research to find out if there is a market for your product or service. The following are a couple of ideas to help you conduct your market research:

• Introduce your product or service at a trade show to see if it generates any interest. If it's something that would benefit local merchants, check out your local Chamber of Commerce to see if it hosts a trade show.

Nearly every industry has some sort of trade show. Rent out booth space and print up some business cards and descriptive flyers to advertise your business idea. Also, be sure to collect contact information of interested parties either through a sign-up list or set out a fish bowl to collect business cards.

- Offer your product or service for free to potential customers in exchange for a frank appraisal of its value, quality, and marketability. Have them either complete a written survey or give you the opportunity to conduct a face-to-face interview.

WRITE A BUSINESS PLAN

Just as you wouldn't walk into a job interview without an updated resume, you should never start out a new business venture without a business plan. A business plan can be as rough or as sophisticated as you deem necessary, depending on whether you plan to be a sole proprietor or the next Bill Gates.

A business plan basically helps you establish, on paper, a clear picture of what your venture is all about. You should state very clear goals and objectives for both now and the future, with time, revenue, and/or volume of business benchmarks in between. Your business plan should include the following components:

- Define your business—its goals and how you plan to achieve them;
- Market analysis—who are your suppliers, customers, and competitors;
- Finances—detail your projected budget, financing, cash flow, and anticipated profits;
- Time tables—benchmarks to serve as guidelines for when you plan to meet specific goals.

Not only will a well-conceived business plan help you organize your new operation, but it is also essential if you plan to apply for financing with a bank or other traditional lender.

ADMINISTRATIVE TASKS

Maybe your new business idea as an entrepreneur is to conduct kayaking tours down the white water river in your area. You envision spending your days out on the water, meeting enthusiastic tourists, and communing with nature on a daily basis.

In reality, you'll spend your evenings in front of a computer and any free time on the phone with vendors and bankers. Many entrepreneurs don't realize just how much time they will have to spend on the more administrative tasks of running their own business. Here are a few examples of just what to expect:

- Banking relationships—checking account, credit cards, applying for financing, investing profits;
- Accounts payable—bill payment, payroll, taxes, supplier invoices, rent, overhead utilities;
- Accounts receivable—keeping track of cash, accepting checks and/or credit cards, establishing payment terms for delinquent customers, dealing with collections or utilizing a collection agency;
- Purchasing—buying or leasing equipment, interviewing suppliers;
- Sales—pricing, marketing, advertising;
- Reporting—cash flow, balance sheets, net worth statements, taxes;
- Professional relationships—bookkeeper, accountant, suppliers, clients.

MARKET YOUR BUSINESS

Unless you've actually worked in a marketing- or sales-oriented position, marketing yourself and finding work can be one of the hardest tasks of running your own business. Fortunately, you are living in one of the best times ever to start out on your own—thanks to the convenience and vast resources of the Internet.

You may set up a Web site to advertise your products or services, and register this site with all the major search domains so that it is included when a user searches for your expertise by keyword. Even better, you may send out an e-mail to potential clients and include a direct link to your Web site location to instantly find out more about your business. No more mailing out a pitch, proposal, or marketing literature and waiting weeks for a response, and having to follow up with phone calls. Generally, if a client is interested in your pitch, you'll hear back within a matter of days or hours.

The following are additional ideas to help you market your home-based business:

- Compile a list of potential customers for your products or services, including their phone numbers, physical and e-mail addresses.

- Call the company to find out who the contact person would be to decide whether or not to use your services, and get their direct contact information.
- When opportunities exist, write a fee proposal that specifies the scope of work, tasks you will perform, a schedule for completion, and your fee as well as a contingency for any unanticipated out-of-pocket expenses.
- Tap old work colleagues and your former employers for both potential work and referrals for new clients.

NETWORK FOR BUSINESS

Who you know is just as important as how good you are as an independent contractor. In fact, it's even more important, since you can't prove your competence if you can't find any clients. Here are a few ideas on how to network your way to a thriving business:

- Join the local Chamber of Commerce and become active in its functions.
- The advantage of pursuing your favorite sport or hobby is that you can expose yourself to a potential network of clients who can see you doing something you love; your passion, discipline, and penchant for hard work will become evident during your encounters. For example:

  - Individual sports—running or walking clubs, the Sierra Club or other recreational organizations, racquetball, squash, tennis, golf, sailing, and skiing.
  - Team sports—baseball, softball, basketball, soccer, volleyball, lacrosse, and hockey.
  - Injury prone?—Try umpiring, refereeing, or coaching your favorite sport.
  - Hobbies—Why not share your passion for cooking or eating by joining a gourmet or dining club? Or indulge your secret desire to learn ballroom dancing, salsa, or swing.

- Get to know people who tend to come in contact with new residents in town, such as real estate agents, contractors, bank tellers, teachers, librarians, hairdressers, and parents at Little League games.

CHEAP (OR FREE) WAYS TO ADVERTISE

- For a small investment of $100–300, sponsor a local team sporting your logo on its jerseys—offering additional exposure to all the league teams and their fans throughout the season. Try to pair your service to the needs of that organization. For example, an adult softball team is likely to require the services of physical therapist or a local bar (for after-game drinks).
- Teach classes in your expertise area at a community college or community center to reach a large range of students, and student referrals.
- Join and/or offer to speak at local community organizations, such as Kiwanis, Ruritan, Junior League, church, or PTA meetings.
- Write articles for local papers or trade newsletters, such as the organizations listed above. Or call/write your local newspaper editor to volunteer your expertise whenever they need sources for articles they are developing.
- Leave a few business cards or post them on bulletin boards at local businesses where potential customers are likely to shop.
- As often as you get a referral, give a referral. Good deeds come back and pay well.

TAXES AND SOCIAL SECURITY

As an independent contractor, you are responsible for paying state and federal taxes on a quarterly basis. While you may not know exactly what you'll earn by the end of the year, the IRS expects you to make a reasonable estimate each quarter and will penalize you if you underestimate your earnings by year-end.

Also, as an independent contractor, you have to pay all of your own Social Security taxes. Both your Social Security and income taxes may be combined into one payment check and submitted with Form 1040 ES in January, April, June, and September of each year.

Despite the financial challenges and potential pitfalls of owning a small or home-based business, the advantages are attractive nonetheless. According to a recent survey of SOHO owners conducted by Working Solo, Inc., the "Four 'F's" ranked highest as the main reasons to launch a SOHO business: Freedom (30%), Flexibility (25%), Fun (12%), and Financial rewards (12%).

Do you have a separate area in your house you use regularly and exclusively for business purposes? Once you deduct all your other expenses, do you have more income than the deductible expenses incurred by your home office?

If your answer is yes to those two questions, you may claim a home office deduction on IRS Form 8829, "Expenses for Business Use of Your Home." However, be aware of the sad, but true, fact that claiming a home office deduction may increase your likelihood of getting audited by the IRS. The home office deduction is one of those perks that send up a red flag, so take pains to make sure yours is legitimate.

WORKING WITH BABY

If you're planning to work from home with a newborn, it's important to recognize the recent changes in your life and don't think everything is going to go back to "normal."

First off, you should prioritize your work and categorize it in terms of (1) what you can do while handling baby (i.e., read while nursing), (2) what you can do while baby is awake but not needing your attention (i.e., light workload), and (3) what you must do while baby is sound asleep (i.e., make phone calls, heavy concentration work).

Next, try to separate work from family life by sticking to a work schedule. It can be tempting to go back to work after dinner when your baby is fast asleep, but this can take its toll on your physical well being. Better to try and stick to your daytime work schedule and maybe take the baby out for a stroll in the early evening. With babies as well as mommies and daddies, schedules become very important and both need plenty of rest as well as fresh air and exercise.

Also, try to take time out for yourself each day, preferably during the transition period between work and family life. Switching gears from dealing with baby spit in your hair to a conference call in no time flat can lead to stress and resentment. Just as you would have a commute period from work to home, take 10–30 minutes for yourself to sit in a quiet corner and reflect peacefully, read non-work-related material, or call a friend. Then you'll feel recharged and can give your baby 100 percent of your attention.

With a home-based business, be prepared to work, work hard, and probably log some long hours. If you need to hold down another "day" job while getting your business off and running, you're going to be strapped for time. Toss in raising your children as a single parent, and now you've signed on to three full-time jobs.

While the long-term rewards may be worth the burden, this is something you might want to think about before you get started down this path.

After all, if the point of extra income is to be able to give more to your family, carefully weigh the trade-off between giving them more of your time versus giving them more money with which to buy stuff.

HEAD OF HOUSEHOLD TIP: WHEN TO START A HOME-BASED BUSINESS

The best time to start a new business venture is, ironically, when you're already out of work. If you expect to be downsized soon, start doing your research now. Once you're out of work, you should split your time between seeking a new position for immediate income replacement and working on your new venture while you have the downtime. If you're totally committed to making your home-based business work, consider alternative job opportunities that may fit your entrepreneur + single parent schedule while still providing income. This may include consulting or seasonal work such as retail during the holidays or tax preparation during the tax season.

PASSIVE INCOME

Unlike a home-based business, which could potentially run you ragged, passive income is exactly what it sounds like: Income you earn while doing nothing, or very little.

"Doing nothing" of course is a relative term, as opposed to working 40 hours a week. Examples of passive residual income include receiving income from rental property you own, royalties on an invention or creative work such as a book, photograph, video, or song, and network marketing, trailed or renewable sales commissions. Passive income is also that generated by a business you own but hire someone else to manage.

Investment income is also considered passive income, as you do the research and decision-making once to create future gains.

BOARDING TENANTS

If you own a sizeable home with extra bedrooms, carefully selecting one or more boarders may be the way to go. If you live in a particularly scenic or touristy area, opening up your home as a Bed & Breakfast can be a way to earn extra income, particularly if you also run a home-based business and are home all day anyway.

Be advised that you may be required to apply each year for a rooming and boarding license and be subject to inspections and record-keeping audits. Check with local and state ordinances before heading down this path.

One of the benefits of renting a room of your home is claiming any related expenses, including home depreciation for the amount of space rented, on your tax return. Of course, you'll also have to include the amount of rental income you received on your return and pay taxes on that money.

INVEST IN REAL ESTATE

Flipping and foreclosure resale aside, real estate is typically considered a "Get Rich Slow" investment. That's generally a good thing. Any scheme that claims it can help you "Get Rich Fast" is probably too good to be true most of the time, and the risk taken may not be worth the potential rewards.

But how do you get started actually making money in real estate? While it certainly helps to have a stash of cash, there are other alternatives. But the first rule of thumb is: Forget those late night get-rich quick schemes you see on TV. With a lot of hard work, you can find properties for sale and flip them quickly for profit. You don't have to pay someone to find those properties for you. The fact is, you can learn much of this information by studying the market on your own.

Even if you have your own capital to invest, it is wise to start small and slowly build your portfolio of real estate properties. Plus, it's less risky to keep your current job and start investing on a part-time basis.

RENTING PROPERTY

The reason owning and managing rental properties can be a slow but lucrative path to wealth is because an investment in single- or multifamily rental properties can appreciate during periods of both inflation and economic strength—simply because underlying property values, occupancy levels, and rental rates tend to continually rise.

The following are three key ways in which owning rental properties can be financially rewarding:

• *Property value appreciation over time*—In order to make money on property appreciation, you'll probably have to hold onto and manage the property for 5–10 years or more.

- *Immediate cash flow*—If you screen and handpick tenants carefully, you can earn regular income to help make loan payments, pay taxes and even property management expenses—which cut into your profit but at least give you more time with your family.
- *Tax shelter*—You may deduct depreciation and management expenses from your income to lower your overall tax bill, including the income earned from renting.

Owning and managing rental property can be an overwhelming responsibility. Just a few of the hassles you may encounter include licensing boards and inspectors, paying for costly repairs and upgrades, and battling unruly tenants who trash your property or are habitually late on their rent.

Even if you hire a property manager to handle your rental properties, you are still likely to have your fair share of migraines.

Investing in Real Estate Equity

I know of one single parent who used the equity in his first, starter house to put a down payment on property three blocks away from the beach. Within six months, property values on this small resort island rose significantly, allowing him to tap the property's equity to build a house on the land. He now rents the beach house and uses the income generated to pay the mortgage, equity loan, taxes, and other expenses—essentially for the house to pay for itself. Over the long term, he will appreciate a high-net asset and/or secure a paid-off beach home for his retirement. He is currently pursuing the same financial strategy with a lakefront property.

FLIPPING FOR CASH

There are three types of real estate "Flippers": Those who seek to buy, those who contract to buy, and those who actually do buy real estate on a regular basis.

The first flipper, also known as a "scout," operates much like a real estate agent. He or she basically seeks out properties and sells them to the type of flipper who actually buys, receiving somewhat of a commission in return. A scout can expect to earn $500–1,000 on each property he or she finds that results in a sale.

The second type of flipper is called a "dealer" and requires a bit more of a commitment. The dealer also locates properties for other investors, but in doing so will first sign a purchase contract with the property owner.

This contract basically says the dealer has the right to buy the property at a certain price. He or she may then go out and sell this contract to a flipper for a slightly higher price, and earn a nice little fee in doing so. The third party will in turn honor the contract and purchase the property at the originally stated price. A full-time dealer can make up to $15,000 a month without ever actually having to buy a piece of property.

Finally, there's the true flipper, a.k.a. the "retailer," who actually buys the property—the one he has either found himself or paid a fee to others to find for him. He may or may not invest money to fix up the property, but the idea is to resell the property for a profit. Naturally, it may take several months to actually resell the property, but the retailer stands to receive greater financial gain than either of the other two types of flippers.

BUYING FORECLOSURES

Thousands of homes end up in foreclosure every year due to economic factors leading to job loss, credit problems, and/or emergency expenses. One way to flip a property for profit is to buy and sell foreclosed properties. Typically, once an owner fails to make three payments toward the mortgage on a property, it is repossessed by the lender and resold. Similar to investing in the stock market, the idea here is to buy cheap and sell high.

You can usually scoop up foreclosed properties at below-value prices. That's because the lender who holds the first loan on the property starts the bidding at the outstanding loan amount—not the full purchase price. Therefore, you may purchase a foreclosed home where the previous owner held significant equity and flip it immediately for the full-value price, squeezing out a tidy profit in the process. That's assuming the auction doesn't run up the sales price to something close to true market value.

However, it can be tough to get financing for this type of real estate investment. You typically have to show up at a foreclosure auction with the full amount of cash you're bidding, or at least a required minimum deposit and proof of a line of credit with your bank upon which you can draw cashier's checks.

The property's condition is typically not well known prior to a foreclosure sale, and in many cases, an interior inspection may not be possible before the sale. Most foreclosed properties are sold "as is," meaning only structural and/or mechanical repairs were made in preparation for the sale.

Foreclosure sales are exempt from some states' disclosure laws, and as a general rule, the law protects the lender who has recently acquired the property through adverse circumstances. So the seller may not be required to disclose all negative aspects of the property as you would expect with a normal sale.

The best way to approach this type of investment is to attend some foreclosure sales and network with the buyers. If you're lucky, you may find one willing to show you the ropes. One place to get started is by checking out HUD foreclosure sales in your area at the U.S. Department of Housing and Urban Development, at www.hud.gov/homes/homes forsale.cfm.

Can you turn real estate investments into full-time income? It takes a lot of time, patience, and hands-on involvement. It is not for the novice or the faint of heart, but it can be done. Once you turn a profit or two and have some working capital of your own, it becomes a matter of opportunity and timing. But best of all, you can work for yourself.

Because you need both time and capital, one of the more opportunistic ways to get started is to use a layoff package, divorce settlement, or some other cash windfall in concert with paid vacation time to make a wise foreclosure purchase.

SELLER FINANCE YOUR REAL ESTATE SALES

When you finance the sale of property that you own, you basically agree to carry back the note. In other words, you become the bank. But instead of receiving the full purchase price up front so you can payoff your loan, you simply finance the deal on credit. While financing the sale of real estate may at first appear to be a risky venture, it in fact offers a multitude of benefits.

For example, seller-financed contracts often command a high down payment, substantially higher interest rates than the going rate, and significantly shorter terms. This allows you to secure a large chunk of cash up front, plus longer-term annuity income that benefits from the tax treatment of an installment sale. Plus, you may even turn around and sell your contract at a discount rate in order to be free and clear of the arrangement.

Seller financing is also a relatively low-risk investment strategy. Rather than investing in low-yielding bonds, you may earn interest rates upward of 8–10 percent from the buyer—a substantial increase over 5 percent. In addition, the risk is actually pretty small when you think about it. If the buyer defaults, he or she loses everything paid into the property, and you basically foreclose on your own property. This allows you to actually make a profit and then resell the property again for additional profit opportunity.

REITS FOR INCOME INVESTORS

Another way to invest for passive income from real estate is to let professional money managers do the work for you. Real Estate Investment Trusts (REITs) fast became the real estate investment of choice during the 1990s. With approximately 125 REITs currently listed on the U.S. stock exchange, they continue to garner healthy respect as a high-income-producing real estate investment.

Better than operating as a landlord, REIT investors buy into a company that generates nearly all of its income from investments in real estate—in particular the direct ownership and operation of property and collection of rental income. While REITs can vary in scope, most invest in a diversified mix of hotels, apartment buildings, industrial properties, office parks, and shopping centers and malls.

Another type of REIT invests purely in mortgages backed by real estate. There are also "hybrids" that invest in both—mortgages and real property.

There are several nice benefits to REIT investing. One is that someone else professionally manages them, much like mutual funds. Also, they tend to provide a stable asset base from rental properties and tend to be much less volatile than stocks or individual real estate holdings. Best of all, REITs must pay out 90 percent of their taxable income to shareholders in the form of dividends, so they provide steady income for investors.

TAX LIEN CERTIFICATES

Hate paying taxes? Become a collector instead. Many U.S. states issue tax lien certificates to investors as a means of garnishing much-needed income.

What this means is that all unpaid property taxes, interest, and penalties due from local taxpayers are balled up into one big debt asset, which is sold to investors at a public auction sale. This is known as a tax lien or tax certificate sale. Once you purchase a tax lien, you have the right to collect the delinquent taxes from the property owner. Keep in mind that the property is not sold, only the right to whom collects the unpaid taxes and fees.

Becoming a collector may seem like a risky prospect, but the yields can be quite high. In Baltimore, Maryland, for instance, lien holders get annualized yields of up to 24 percent. About 15 other states boast yields ranging from 14 to 20 percent.

Better yet, tax certificates are secured by the local government and are generally the first lien on the property. In other words, if the property must be sold to pay off debts, you're assured to be the first one in line for payment.

To learn more about tax lien sales in your area, visit county Web sites.

DIVORCED SPOUSE SOCIAL SECURITY BENEFITS

The most important time to enjoy passive income is during retirement, so ensure you are aware of all of your potential resources.

This includes retirement income. Many times a stay-home mom finds herself in a particularly sticky situation. After years of maintaining a home and raising children, she finds herself divorced, living on substantially less income composed of alimony and child support, and has no marketable work skills or experience with which she can convert into a substantial living of her own.

To qualify for Social Security benefits in retirement, an individual needs at least 40 credits (quarters) of work history in which Social Security taxes were paid. This equates to about 10 years of work history. Let's say a woman marries at age 30, having worked for 8 years, then becomes a home-maker for the next 30 to raise the couples' brood. She finds herself at age 60, divorced from her husband, with no substantial work history and no Social Security benefits of her own.

There are two categories of Social Security benefits: That which is earned by the employed spouse, and a "derivative" benefit to which a non-employed or lower-wage spouse is entitled.

The following are basic guidelines for divorcee benefits based on the primary wage earner's work history:

- You must have been married for at least 10 years;
- Ex-spouse benefits are gender neutral; husband or wife may receive benefits based on the highest wage earner;
- The ex-spouse is entitled to either his or her individual earned benefit *or* the derivative benefit—whichever is higher;
- If one ex-spouse does not have a substantial work history, the benefits for both are based on the primary worker's lifetime contribution, not just during the years the couple was married;
- The ex-spouse applying for derivative benefits must not remarry (although eligibility can be reinstated if a subsequent marriage ends in divorce);
- The number of spousal benefits has no bearing on the worker's benefits, even if a string of ex-wives are eligible for benefits;

• Neither ex-spouse may apply for benefits until the primary worker reaches minimum retirement age.

Should you become a single parent by way of a spouse dying, as long as you are raising the deceased's child who is younger than age 16 or disabled, you may qualify to receive Social Security benefits.

LOSS OF INCOME

Should you lose your current income, don't hesitate to contact your mortgage lender, creditors, and utility companies to let them know you're temporarily unemployed. Rather than waiting for overdue bills to pour in, you can proactively negotiate temporary plans for reduced payments.

In many cases, you can negotiate and, in some cases, get a forbearance agreement with your bank or mortgage company that will allow you to pay a fraction of your mortgage until you find a new job or income source. This will not reduce your loan, but it will allow you to take control of the situation and reduce household bills on a short-term basis.

EIGHT

Insurance

Insurance can feel like a necessary evil. Something you spend money on for years and years and for which you never receive goods or a return on your investment—and that's if you're lucky. It's such a bizarre concept.

All insurance is based on a risk pool. Basically, if you get enough people to pitch in, claims can be covered by the many instead of burdening the few. As such, healthy people pay for the claims of the chronically sick. And good drivers pay for damages caused by bad drivers. It's simply the way insurance works.

So in a sense, it is a necessary evil. Because the things insurance covers—like your home, your car, your life—are big-ticket items. It's not likely you would be able to replace them on your own without insurance.

Insurance is especially important for the single parent. Obviously, with only one income, replacing that income many times over if you were to die is crucial to your children's future. The same holds true for most of the other items for which insurance policies are offered.

You cut costs where you can, but like health insurance, this isn't an area where a single parent can cut corners.

LIFE INSURANCE

First and foremost, make sure your family is protected in the event of your death with life insurance. Many employers provide life insurance as part of their benefits package but pay close attention to how much they offer. It is usually two or three times your annual salary, which won't amount to much if you don't make a lot of money—particularly true when you're just starting out in your career.

And consider that two times your annual salary really only amounts to about two years of expenses for whomever becomes guardian to your children. If you have a little one, or even an older one bound for college, that money isn't going to last long.

As a head of household, you may need to take out additional insurance coverage because you have no income-earning partner capable of providing for your family after you're gone. Basically, your children will go to your guardian, and your life insurance money will be used to help raise them. Make sure you have enough to get them through their teenage years and send them to college, as this would be an additional hardship if whoever cares for your children has to bear this unexpected and unplanned for expense.

As far as coverage amounts go, as a rule of thumb, seek coverage of between five and seven times your annual income. As far as the various types of policies go, they can generally be broken down into one of two categories: Term and Permanent.

Term Insurance

Term insurance generally provides coverage for a specified period of time and pays out a specified amount of coverage to your beneficiary only if you die within that time period. You pay the same amount of premium from the first day of the policy until the term ends. Term is typically the most popular type of insurance policy because it gives you the largest immediate death benefit for the lowest amount of premium, especially for people under 30 years old.

Permanent Insurance

Permanent insurance does not need to be renewed, as a policy will stay in effect permanently for the rest of your life as long as premiums continue to be paid. There are two types of permanent insurance policies: Whole Life and Universal Life.

Whole Life is designed to cover your whole life and offers the ability to build up cash value in addition to paying out a death benefit. Like term insurance, the premium you pay remains level throughout the life of the policy. However, you start out paying a higher premium than you would for term coverage, but that amount will end up being less than what you would have to pay for term coverage as you get older.

Part of your premium will go toward administrative expenses and the death benefit, and part of it will grow in a tax-deferred, fixed rate cash account from which you may withdraw or borrow against as needed.

Universal Life also offers the cash account option as well as a flexible premium. This means that when you have extra money on hand, you may apply it to your contract to help build up your cash value. And when you are short of cash, you may actually skip a premium payment now and then as long as your cash account has built up enough to cover the cost of insurance and expenses.

With a Variable Universal Life policy, you may select how the funds in the cash value portion of the policy are invested by choosing from an array of investment options, including stocks, bonds, and/or money market mutual funds, for potentially higher growth. As time goes on, you may transfer money in and out of investment options based on changes in your personal or financial situation, or in reaction to current market conditions—without incurring taxes.

It's important to note that both whole life and universal life policies are significantly more expensive than term life policies. And, if you skip too many payments, you may cause your universal life policy to lapse.

You shouldn't name your underage children as your beneficiaries of your life insurance and investment accounts, as someone else will have to manage the money on their behalf. In fact, if your children are not of legal age upon your death, an insurance company cannot release the money directly to them. That's why it's important to select a guardian for your children; this guardian should be your named beneficiary on these accounts.

Alternately, you may select a custodian to manage your children's assets until they come of age. In this case, you would name the children as policy beneficiaries and name a custodian under the Uniform Transfer to Minors Act (UTMA) or Uniform Gifts to Minors Act (UGMA). A custodian has the fiduciary responsibility to manage the account for your children's benefit. For a life insurance policy, you should write "(Name of Custodian), as Custodian for (Name of Minor) under the (Name of State) UTMA."

Money in a custodial account legally belongs to the minor but is controlled by the custodian until the child reaches the age specified by the account. UTMA custodianship generally ends at either age 18 or 21 (depending on the state). If you don't want your children to receive proceeds so young, you may want to establish a trust instead, in which you may specify at what age (over 18) or under what conditions you wish the money to be distributed.

HEAD OF HOUSEHOLD TIPS: BUYING LIFE INSURANCE

Unlike buying a car or a bar of soap, it's tough to know what you're getting with life insurance. In fact, you may never find out—but your loved ones sure will once you pass away. Follow these guidelines to help you purchase a policy that meets your individual needs:

- Don't just buy the cheapest policy; check out the company. Consumer publications or A. M. Best (www.ambest.com), a well-respected analyst, can give you ratings for the financial stability and claims-paying record of various insurers.

- Comparison shop. This is easier than ever to do today, thanks to online sites that procure multiple quotes for you in record time. Check out www.insure.com or www.netquote.com.

- Make sure you compare apples to apples. Policies can be layered and complex, so ensure you ask for the same type and level of coverage to make an accurate rate comparison.

- The purpose of life insurance is to protect those who would suffer financially if you died, so calculate the amount of coverage you would need to meet this goal, taking into consideration any benefits provided by Uncle Sam.

- As a general rule, people in their early twenties and in their sixties or older have less need for life insurance coverage; people with minor children have a far greater need. Single parents have the greatest need.

LONG-TERM CARE INSURANCE

How many times have you thought to yourself, "That'll never happen to me?" Before you conclude that you have enough health care insurance, consider that nearly 50 percent of Americans age 65 and over will spend some time in a nursing home, and one in four Americans are expected to require an *extended stay* in a nursing home.

Long-term care insurance consists of coverage for a wide range of services, including nursing-home care, assisted-care facilities, and even in-home care. Long-term care may take the form of rehabilitative care for someone recovering from a heart attack or stroke, custodial care and supervision for a cognitively impaired person suffering from Alzheimer's disease, or personal care for someone who is physically disabled.

Long-term care is best covered by insurance—not personal savings. Today, nearly half of the people in nursing homes are forced to drain their retirement savings and, in many cases, the financial resources of their families.

Why is this particular expense important to today's single parents? Because people are living longer than ever—including your parents. Sure, that active 65-year-old in your den playing UNO with your children may be fully coherent now, but in 10 years (about the time you need to pay for college), this might not be the case. In fact, your parents may live longer, but that doesn't mean they'll be 100 percent physically and cognitively healthy.

Here's a typical scenario for the twenty-first century: Imagine you are 45 years old and have a deteriorating senior parent (or two) who really needs to move out of the single-family home into a group home for 24-hour access to assistance. This is about the time your first child, the motivated one who studied and made good grades, got into an expensive out-of-state college and needs you to help pay for his or her education. Meanwhile, you've got one or more preteens or teenagers at home driving you crazy with the mouth, the entitled attitude, lower grades, and the sketchy friends who keep you up at night with worry. And if you're not already a single parent, mid-forties is a popular age for divorce, further depleting family finances and resources. Oh, and let's talk about your job. Inexperienced twenty-something MBAs are being hired at salaries above what's taken you a lifetime to achieve, while you're receiving lateral and "perception" demotions, lower salary increases, and finally, you're laid off for making too much money with no long-term leadership prospects.

Welcome to the twenty-first century (and they wonder why the economy crashed in 2008).

These new-age issues are hard enough for a two-income family. But to face them alone as a single parent? Good grief.

You've got one thing going for you though, and it is truly invaluable. You've already been through tough times as a single parent and have survived. Single parents are resourceful, resilient, and independent-minded. You'll get through this, like you have everything else. Failure is not an option.

However, knowing your insurance and financial options is paramount, especially when it comes to taking care of your aging parents and, eventually, yourself.

Don't make the mistake of relying on the government for long-term care requirements. Medicare serves as insurance against the costs of acute care only, for which the goal is short-term recovery. As a result, when Medicare does pay for long-term care, it is related to rehabilitation arising from an acute medical condition.

The government program that does fund long-term care—Medicaid—requires that the recipient deplete most of his or her assets before it will pay long-term care bills. In recent years, several proposals to create a federal insurance program for long-term care have been introduced, but none have succeeded.

The younger you buy a long-term care policy—for yourself or your parents—the lower the premium cost. If you wait too late, your elderly parent may not qualify for coverage due to a preexisting condition.

When choosing a particular insurer or long-term care policy, consider the company's financial stability (check its industry rating) and experience offering long-term care insurance, as well as the policy's varying levels of care, community-based benefits, choice, and flexibility. How policies pay out benefits may vary. Indemnity policies pay a fixed dollar amount each day the policy owner receives covered care; $100 a day is common. Some policies may only cover a certain percentage of the costs associated with various services. Still, other policies may pay a specific dollar amount to cover the actual charges for covered services received.

Men and women of the same age pay the same premium; there is no gender differential. One way to reduce premiums is to select a longer elimination period. This is the waiting period before a policy owner may begin collecting benefits; 90–100 days is common.

Here's a list of oft-overlooked pitfalls to avoid in long-term care insurance policies:

- Insurance premiums that increase with age;
- Home health benefits not provided or only after receiving nursing-home care;
- Hospitalization or skilled care that must occur before benefits are paid;
- A clause that specifies the policy is renewable only under certain conditions;
- A maximum benefit period of less than two years;

- Deductible or waiting period exceeding 100 days;
- Policies that do not include skilled, intermediate, and custodial nursing care;
- Policies that exclude coverage for mental or nervous disorders (like Alzheimer's);
- A "preexisting condition clause" of longer than six months.

A good rule of thumb is to purchase a long-term care policy before age 55 in order to get a lower premium. It's important to buy coverage before you or your parents are diagnosed with a long-term illness. However, other conditions—such as controlled hypertension or a history of cancer—won't necessarily disqualify a candidate from coverage.

Consider this: If you have a million or more dollars, you can afford long-term care on your own. If you are dirt poor, Medicaid will cover your long-term care. But, if you're middle income, long-term care may wipe out everything you have worked for your entire lifetime.

Long-term care insurance is designed to protect you from the financial burdens associated with an extended illness or nursing-home stay. Because when illness strikes, coping with emotional stress is tough enough—you shouldn't have to worry about draining your family's savings.

HOMEOWNER'S INSURANCE

When you buy a home, your mortgage lender is going to require that you take out a homeowner's insurance policy on your new home. This is to protect their investment as much as yours.

Your bank or mortgage company may require you to purchase coverage up to the amount that it would cost to rebuild your home in the event of fire or some other calamity. But that amount of coverage won't be enough. Just imagine how much it would cost you to replace everything in the house as well. You should be prepared to fork out a higher premium for enough coverage to replace both the structure and all of your possessions.

One homeowner's insurance pitfall to watch out for is coverage for "cash value" versus "replacement cost." This is the difference between getting $30 for a 10-year-old television and $400 for a new one. Your old TV may only be worth $30 on the used TV market, but how on earth can you possibly replace it with only $30 coverage? Be sure and get "replacement cost" coverage for your possessions, while "actual cash value" should work fine for rebuilding the house itself.

Homeowner's insurance carriers typically offer a multitude of different types of policies, spanning a large price range. Most policies include liability coverage, which pays for injuries to other people or damages you cause to their property, up to certain limits. The following is a basic guide used in most states that can help you determine the level of coverage you need:

The HO-1 is a basic homeowner's policy that covers your house and possessions against 11 different perils, including fire, smoke, vandalism, windstorm, theft/burglary, and riot/civil commotion. HO-1 insurance also covers medical liability and personal liability. Additionally, the policy typically includes coverage of damage done to other people's property, living expenses if your home is damaged, legal defense in liability cases, and personal property both at home and while traveling.

An HO-1 policy does not cover flooding—that requires separate coverage only offered through the government.

HO-2 is a broader homeowner's policy that covers your house and its contents against 17 perils, including damage from snow, ice, or a falling object. This policy's premiums are typically 5–10 percent higher than those of an HO-1 policy.

- HO-3—is a special homeowner's policy that covers all perils except those specifically excluded by the policy.
- HO-5—is an extensive homeowner's policy that covers damage from nearly everything but floods, earthquakes, and wars.
- HO-6—is for owners of co-ops or condominiums: Insurance provided by the owner's association normally covers most of the actual structure; this type of policy covers personal property and liability.
- HO-8—provides repair costs or actual cash value coverage, typically purchased for older homes that are paid for.

Premiums for homeowner's insurance can vary substantially between carriers, so it pays to shop around. Be prepared to offer up the following information to help your representative quote an accurate premium: What is the home's . . .

- Composition (wood, brick, vinyl siding, etc.)
- Date it was built
- Location
- Square footage

- Number of rooms
- Heat source
- Number of people to reside there
- Proximity to the nearest fire station and fire hydrant

You will also be asked questions about proactive maintenance that can actually lower your premium, such as whether or not the home has an alarm system, smoke detectors, or dead bolt locks. Another way you can get a rate discount is to purchase your life, auto, and homeowner's policies all from the same company. Keep in mind, too, that the higher the policy deductible, the lower the premium.

Factors that can increase your homeowner's premium include if you're a smoker, whether you own certain breeds of dogs, if you have an in-ground pool or a trampoline, if you have a poor credit rating, or if the home is located in a higher risk area, such as a coastline.

It also helps to take an overall inventory of your possessions—in terms of replacement costs—so you know how much coverage you need when you request a quote. An easy way to do this is to take photos or videotape each room, and take down the serial numbers for items like a computer. This will come in handy for theft recovery.

An added bonus to some homeowner's insurance policies is that they cover unauthorized use of credit cards and off-premises theft protection should your hotel room get robbed while on vacation.

Today, the insurance industry is plagued by depressed financial markets and the expensive claims of recent years. This scenario has produced higher premiums and has even made it tougher for new home buyers to get insurance coverage. If you find you're unable to buy insurance anywhere else, investigate your state's Fair Access to Insurance Requirement (www.iii.org) plan—a last resort that offers limited coverage at higher rates.

RENTER'S INSURANCE

If you rent, don't make the mistake of assuming your belongings are covered by your landlord's insurance policy for the building. An owner's policy will cover the cost of repairing, replacing, or rebuilding the structure and interior elements of a rental unit. Not the renter's personal possessions.

Most renters don't even consider buying property insurance until they're ready to buy a home. But what if something should happen to your stuff—your furniture, clothes, and valuables—could you afford to replace it all? Renter's insurance generally charges a small, affordable premium each month or each year in return for insuring the replacement value of your personal possessions.

The HO-4 policy is designed for renters and covers losses from 17 types of perils, including fire, smoke damage, lightning, hail, falling aircraft, vehicles, vandalism, theft, and water-related damage from home utilities (but again, not flooding).

And as with homeowner's insurance, you want to be sure your renter's policy covers replacement value—not just the actual cash value. Otherwise, you may not get enough money to cover the purchase of new items, particularly if the originals were old.

Some policies also cover "additional living expenses." Generally, this means that if your apartment is damaged so badly that you must temporarily live elsewhere, the policy will pay for your short-term relocation expenses.

Most renter insurance policies also cover liability. This means it'll pay for any medical expenses, up to certain limits, incurred by a visitor who, for example, slips on a rug and breaks her leg.

As with all insurance policies, the purpose of renter's insurance is to cover losses you cannot afford. You may think you don't need a renter's policy, but you may wish you had one the moment you discover you've been robbed.

U.S. statistics show that renters experience higher rates of property crime than do homeowners, so you're actually at greater risk. However, renter's rates are significantly less than homeowner's policies because they don't cover the cost of the building itself. Many policies cost less than $200 per year—under $20 a month—for $12,000–15,000 of replacement cost coverage and $100,000 of liability insurance. That monthly premium may be more than a compact disk, but the annual premium typically costs less than an entire stereo system.

AUTO INSURANCE

Way back in your younger days, maybe you had an accident or a fender bender, got a few speeding tickets, and your CD player was stolen when you forgot to lock your car. While those are all factors that can influence your auto insurance premiums, they're in the past. You're more mature now; haven't had a wreck or a speeding ticket in nearly a decade.

However, in recent years, a new trend in auto insurance rates can hurt you just as much at 25 or 45 years of age. That's because auto insurance premiums are now influenced by your credit history.

Credit scores are determined by such factors as how much debt you carry and whether you make payments on time. And if you've recently filed for bankruptcy, gotten a divorce, or lost your job, these same factors that affect your credit score can now impact how much you have to pay for auto insurance.

An increasingly popular trend in the insurance industry is to use a consumer's credit report to justify raising auto premiums, place you in a higher-priced policy, and even cancel your car insurance altogether. Apparently, research has revealed that there is a correlation between people with low credit scores and people who file auto claims. Interestingly enough, the correlation isn't related to having accidents—but rather to the act of filing claims afterward.

This can best be explained with an example. How often do you hear of people paying out of pocket for damages from a fender bender rather than filing a claim with their insurance company? How often have you heard someone complain that, despite a perfect driving record, their insurance rates went through the roof after they filed a claim related to an accident that wasn't even their fault—such as damage from hitting a deer? In this day and age, the better long-term solution is not to file a claim if you can reasonably pay for the damage out of pocket.

With credit scoring, insurance companies believe they are closer to profiling the type of person who will file a claim based on their financial management skills. That's not just bad drivers either—it's drivers whose cars are burglarized or vandalized. Drivers who file claims, no matter how small, rather than covering small expenses themselves are the target market for higher auto insurance rates.

Credit scores are based on information contained in consumer credit reports from Equifax, Experian, and TransUnion. In addition to these scores, insurance companies look at the driver's motor vehicle records, loss reports, and application information to determine insurance risk.

Obey the Easy Rules

I, for one, cannot explain how auto insurance premiums are actually determined. But I can share my experience. When my eldest son turned 16, my auto insurance premiums doubled. And after he got his first ticket, I thought they would go through the roof. When he got his second ticket, I anticipated nothing less than financial ruin. Now granted, the child did suffer through traffic school both times, but I didn't honestly think that would stop our auto insurance rates from rising. Nonetheless, our rates *never rose; not once. In fact, one month before he turned 21, I received a revised annual premium: $300 less than I had previously been paying.*

Are the gods smiling on me? On some things I think they are, but I don't think they waste their time on adjusting my auto insurance rates. Here's the only practical explanation I can offer: My son and I both drive cars more than 10 years old. We both have bumps and dings that we generally shrug off and ignore without fear of social rejection. My minivan in fact, with its four-cylinder engine and relatively good gas mileage, does not have automatic locks or windows. I like to think I'm getting a bicep workout as a result. I also do not suffer from periodic electrical repairs, as do many car owners with the latest bells and whistles. Yay. But is our careless attitude with regard to vehicle vanity the reason why my auto insurance rates didn't skyrocket? Even during those irascible teenage years?

I don't know, but I have a theory. I personally consider the purpose of a vehicle as a means of transporting my family from point A to point B. My car shopping concerns are primarily focused on safety, reliability, and yes, gas mileage. Sporty looks, not an issue. I don't fix dents and scratches (honestly, I don't even notice them until my father points them out).

I suspect this innate inattention to car detailing has to do with my relatively nonmaterialistic set of values (with some exceptions). And remarkably, though inadvertently, my passive attitude has passed on to my son, who cruised through his teenage years devoid of inner longings for a cool sports car. The one issue, however, with which I actively harangue him about is to be solicitous of the rules of the road, the rules of propriety, and of course, the rules that brush up against the law.

My advice to him is simple: Obey the rules. To me, it makes life so much simpler to go the speed limit, not make illegal U-turns, park in legal zones, etc. Having raised two "illegitimate" (who makes these rules?) children on my own for nearly the whole of my adult life, I have intimate and first-hand experience of the ramifications of going against the grain, pushing the envelope, breaking the mold of societal-driven expectations. But I find in order to lead a unique, independent, and purpose-driven life, occasionally you must make somewhat controversial decisions. In light of these contentious, life-altering choices, minding a sign that reads "15-minute parking" seems a small act to concede.

Empirical evidence suggests it doesn't hurt your auto insurance rates either.

Be aware that sometimes when you apply for auto insurance coverage, you'll be quoted one price initially, but once the company has had time to review your application and pull your credit report, it may raise the rate. This "bait and switch" practice often results in either you being forced to pay a higher premium than expected or forfeiting the down payment you sent in with your application.

Surprisingly, auto insurance is one of those industries where shopping around can make a big difference. Prices may vary for the exact same coverage from company to company—sometimes by as much as hundreds of dollars.

Experts advise that you should get at least three different quotes before you make your final decision. And make sure you're comparing apples to apples—don't let one company get by with a higher deductible or lower coverage unless you ask all the quoting companies to do the same. Also, don't forget that service is just as important as price. Premiums tend to rise through the years no matter which company you choose, so make sure you start with a company you can live with regardless.

And so it goes with insurance: The higher your deductible, the lower your premium payments. In the auto insurance biz, lowering your deductible on collision and comprehensive coverage can reduce your premiums substantially.

For example, say you increase your deductible from $200 to $500. The result can range from a 15 to 30 percent reduction in your premium. So consider how much you can reasonably afford to pay out in a lump sum as your deductible in an emergency situation. Then compare that amount to how much you would save on a monthly basis with a lower premium.

Most of all, don't be shy about asking for premium payment ranges based on varying deductibles: There's no shame in making your insurance agent work for his or her commission.

The older your car gets, the less valuable it is and therefore less expensive to repair. The good news is that it is generally less costly to insure. For example, an older car worth less than $1,000 hardly rates a deductible of $1,000. In this case, consider dropping collision and comprehensive (fire and theft) insurance altogether, maintaining only liability coverage (mandatory in most states).

Why pay for coverage that's worth more than the car? Once your car is 10 years or older, check out its book value by visiting www.kbb.com (Kelley Blue Book) to see if this is an economical option. After all, there should be some perk to driving around in an older car.

Keep in mind, however, if you're making payments on a car loan, the lien holder will probably require you to carry comprehensive coverage.

If you're in the market to buy a new car (or a used car that will be new to you), check out the cost of insuring the car(s) you are considering.

Some cars are expensive to repair, and some are particularly prone to theft. Consequently, they are more expensive to insure.

Go online to one of the many auto insurance quote sites and plug in information about the car(s) you are considering to compare insurance rates. And, like most things in life, with auto insurance you really have to ask to get the best deal. This includes discount offers, which aren't always obvious to the buyer. The easiest way to find out what discounts are available is to simply ask an insurance agent or broker. If he or she needs a little prodding, consider the following discounts offered by many of the major auto insurers across the country.

- Low or restricted mileage (good if you work at home or at least nearby);
- Cars equipped with automatic seat belts or air bags;
- Cars equipped with antilock brakes;
- Good driver discounts if you haven't had an accident in the past three years;
- Multicar discounts for insuring more than one car with the same insurer;
- Multiple-policy discounts if you also get homeowner's insurance with the same company;
- Loyalty discounts if you've been with the same company for a certain number of years;
- Driver training courses; particularly for new teenage drivers;
- Cars equipped with antitheft devices, such as alarms, wheel locking devices, window ID systems, and ignition and fuel cutoff systems;
- Nonsmoker discounts;
- Drivers over a certain age, such as 25 or 50;
- Carpooling discounts;
- College students away from home without a car;
- Teenage drivers may receive a good student discount with proof of a minimum grade point average.

DOES YOUR CHILD NEED LIFE INSURANCE?

Although agents may try to sell these policies to you, children seldom have a need for life insurance. Your money would be better invested in a college savings account from which you would retain the money should something happen to your child.

The one exception is if your child provides vital income for the family, as in the case of a child actor or model. As with parents, the rule of thumb in this scenario is to cover your child between five and seven times his or her annual income.

NINE

Investing

Children, ah children. Those money siphons of need and greed. And here we are, struggling single parents, wanting to give them all that they desire and more. Sigh.

To make it worse, it would appear that there are more games to play than ever before. Board games, video games, sports games. That means there's more to buy. There are more restaurants. More stores. An entirely new (online) medium for shopping. More more more.

You need to provide, you need to save. You need to invest. You have short-term goals, such as a car or a house, and you have long-term goals like providing college educations and your own retirement.

These priorities are hard enough to juggle with a two-income family. With a one-income married couple, very difficult. Single-income single parent? Darn nearly impossible.

Nearly.

Where to get started is simple. Determine your goals, both long-term and short-term, and calculate how much money you will need to achieve them.

How to achieve your goals? Well, this is something different entirely.

THE BIG DILEMMA

Financial experts say you've got to invest for retirement. But they also say you've got to pay off all of your credit card debt. For cash-strapped single parents, this conflicting advice provides the makings of a migraine.

Let's face it: Until you get credit card debt under control, it's like digging a hole in the surf: the empty space gets filled up as soon as you create it. So here's the big dilemma . . . how do you prioritize paying off debt *and* investing for the future when you have limited funds?

One way to get started is to put at least a smidgen of your paycheck into your company's 401(k) plan (403(b) if you work in education or 457 if you work for a government agency). It probably won't seem like investing, because you don't have to learn anything, or buy or sell anything, or even speak with a broker. You might just end up picking out a couple of fund choices with the prettiest names.

The younger you are, the more suitable it is to reject fund names that included the words government and bond—another word for debt, which should naturally turn your stomach. As a general rule, these fund choices are too conservative for a young person. Fund names with the words growth and blue chip are positive, accessible names that imply long-term growth. The longer term you have before you need to tap retirement money (10+ years), the more of these fund names you'll want to select.

You should consider investing this smidgen even if you are plugging away at credit card payments. Eventually you will discover a funny thing that happens on the way to T. J. Maxx—my metaphorical image for spending money unnecessarily. If you begin reading your quarterly 401(k) statements, you'll be amazed at how quickly your account balance can grow—what with your paltry contributions and the company match.

At the very least, your growth will be modest but consistent. Even when your lovely funds lose money, your account value will continue to rise because you constantly contribute money each paycheck.

The Tale of Nellie Walker

You may find you are so motivated by watching your 401(k) investment grow that you'll want to open a separate mutual fund account of your own, kind of like Nellie Walker.

Nellie, a single mom in her late twenties, worked as an assistant account manager for a software company. When she was promoted to account manager, she used her salary increase to open a non-retirement mutual fund account. It had a cosmopolitan name: Worldwide.

Then Nellie switched employers. Her old 401(k) slowly waned over the next few months; no doubt missing her constant contributions. So she decided to open an IRA and made a direct transfer of money from her old 401(k) into this new account—the mutual fund company showed her how to do it properly so she wouldn't get clobbered with taxes.

The stock market did well that year, and her IRA index fund—invested primarily in the largest capitalized stock on the American stock exchanges—made more than 30 percent that year. For Nellie, this was a killing when you consider she did nothing more than make a decision to transfer money from her old 401(k).

But Nellie was also experiencing the big dilemma. She was wallowing in debt but enjoying this ride down the avenues of investing. She was so excited by the prospect of earning money that she became downright miserly. No more trips to T. J. Maxx. In fact, she cut back on a lot of things. She threw work bonuses at credit card debts and raised her 401(k) contribution every time she got a raise. She treated herself to opening a new mutual fund with one of those wonderful names every few years. A funny thing happened by her mid-thirties: Not only were her debts paid off, but Nellie had a bona fide investment portfolio.

So yes, financial experts will tell you to pay off your debts first. But just remember how the surf rushes to fill your footprints as you walk along the shore. Clearing off credit card debt is just an invitation to charge more. What really must be accomplished is a change in lifestyle, in mind-set. And the best way to gain this mind-set is to have some success, however limited, watching money grow. Even with debt in hand, it's very comforting to also have a net worth. You shouldn't just be in debt; investing will help teach you how to save and conserve money for long-term goals. In short, investing can help motivate you to get out of debt faster.

Watching money grow is as effortless as watching it diminish. The more success you have, the more you crave. You won't experience this feverish sensation in any activity that has to do with debt. It's tough to cut back on life's little necessaries such as new lipstick or a necktie if all you gain is few bucks less in credit card debt.

Learn what Nellie learned. You must invest to break through the misappropriation of funds that is the big dilemma. If single parents believe they have to pay off credit cards first, given the complexity and juggled priorities that our lives hold, we may never invest or start way too late.

Invest while you're young, when you can still make millions. Start with your company plan, open an IRA, invest in a mutual fund. Learn to replace the thrill of a year-end sale with the thrill of a year-end contribution. In the end, your credit cards will thank you.

INVESTMENT CONCEPTS

The Hare versus the Tortoise: Starting Young

You can forge your own financial security with a plan, a little discipline, and not buying so much coffee. No doubt you've heard the story about the hare and the tortoise, who plodded along slowly but tenaciously and won the footrace while the much faster hare ran hither dither. Most folks fall into one of these two categories when it comes to money: those who have a plan, and those who don't (the "hither dithers").

What's fortunate for a newly emancipated college graduate is that he or she has the opportunity to forge a plan for long-term prosperity. This is something not even his or her parents can match if they didn't start a plan at that age.

The first fundamental of this plan is to learn what you must have and what you can live without. This way, even those starting out at low-level, low-income jobs can still find a way to invest on a regular basis. For many, this means learning to avoid the gourmet coffee habit, planning meals, and taking leftovers to work for lunch. These simple tasks can save $25 or more a week.

There's an added bonus, for what it's worth. Food experts say there is a positive correlation between people who actually cook in their kitchen with those who maintain a healthy weight. In other words, if you eat out a lot, you're more likely to gain weight, not to mention all the extra money you spend.

Many mutual funds will allow you to open an account with as little as $250. You can also set up a monthly automatic transfer program from your checking account to your mutual fund account. So as you can see, you don't have to have a lot of money to become an investor, you just need regular income and a little self-discipline.

Dollar-Cost Averaging

By setting aside a tiny portion of your income each month, you may take advantage of an investment technique called dollar-cost aver-aging. This is when you invest the same amount of money each month—preferably automatically—so it goes straight from your bank account to the investment of your choice, including a 401(k), 457, or 403(b) plan.

This is how dollar-cost averaging works and why it's a successful investment technique. Say you invest $100 a month for six months.

The share price of your investment fluctuates each month, and you pay $6, $9, $10, $9, $8, and $10 per share, respectively, during the six-month period. It's easier to look at this example in a table, as follows:

Table D   Dollar-Cost Averaging Table

Amount invested each month ($)	Share price each month ($)	Number of shares purchased each month
100	6	16.16
100	9	11.11
100	10	10.00
100	9	11.11
100	8	12.50
100	10	10.00
Total invested: $600	**Average Share Price: $8.66**	**Total shares purchased: 70.88**

While the average share price was $8.66, your average cost per share was even lower: $8.46. You calculate the cost by dividing the total $600 invested by the number of shares purchased (70.88). The result is an actual cost of $8.46 per share.

That 20¢ less per share may not seem like much, but the disparity grows much greater the longer you continue this investment plan. This lower cost is almost always evident when you dollar-cost average over time.

Amassing a Fortune

While investing a little at a time may not seem like much, the earlier you start the more you can take advantage of the long-term magic of interest compounding. There is no greater advantage to investing than simply time—a long-term investment horizon.

Starting small, miniscule in fact, is fine. The key is starting.

To see how effective this can be, say you're able to invest $150 a month for the next 10 years. Committing that much money right now may sound like a big deal, but consider how little it will seem when you're making two or three times your current salary later on in your career. At a conservative 5 percent average annual percentage rate of return, you would accumulate about $23,500—easily a down payment on a home. And much more than that if you continue to increase your investment amounts each time you receive a salary increase.

The following are several key ingredients to your long-term financial success. Keep them in mind as you make new decisions in your life such as how expensive an apartment to rent or house to buy, whether or not to buy clothes that require dry cleaning, and how many trips to Target it really takes to equip your home.

- Your first savings priority, before you even begin an investment plan, is to stash away two to three months worth of living expenses. In fact, the earlier you are in your career, the more you can consider yourself one of the first to go should your company require layoffs. Plus, you never know when you may need this money for emergencies . . . and that's just what you're saving it for.
- If you haven't done so already, apply for a credit card but use it wisely. Whenever you make a credit purchase, set aside money in your checking account to pay off the balance each month. Your perpetual goal, no matter how many times you fail to meet it due to necessity, is to never spend more than you can afford to pay off that month.
- As soon as you can, enroll in your company's 401(k) or similar retirement plan. The combination of tax-deferred compounding and any match your company makes adds up to free money in your account. You invest a little, and the match and interest add even more. It's more lucrative than saving.
- Recognize the importance of opening up some other type of investment plan, be it mutual funds or a stock portfolio, in addition to your company's retirement plan. Because you can't touch designated retirement plan money before age $59\frac{1}{2}$ without being subject to a 10 percent penalty fee, it's important to have a second plan in place you can tap when it comes time to put a down payment on a house, pay for college, or bankroll your own business.
- Mutual funds generally offer more market risk protection than a stock portfolio because they are typically more diversified. They're also a good place for a novice investor to start because professional money managers manage them, so investment decisions aren't left up to you.

Asset Allocation

Did you know that the types of assets in which you invest determine how your investment will perform? Not when you invest—and not in which particular stocks or bonds you invest. It's the specific combination of investment classes in which you invest money that will have the most impact on your investment's overall return.

Asset allocation is the strategy of investing your money across a variety of different asset classes—such as stocks, bonds, and cash instruments—as opposed to simply diversifying holdings within one particular asset class. That because when one aspect of the market declines, some or all of portfolio losses may be offset by the performance of other investment categories on the rise.

There are three main investment categories, also known as asset classes. They are

- Stocks—represent ownership in a company, and generally offer the best growth opportunities over the long term
- Bonds—represent your loan to a government or corporation, and generally offer steady interest income
- Cash—represent short-term instruments like a money market account, and provide more downside protection for your investment but less growth potential

The best strategy is to spread your money across some combination of these three investment categories. How much you put into each category is really the decision that requires the most time and consideration.

Generally, riskier investments offer higher return potential. By investing in all three categories, you combine riskier investments (stocks) with moderate-risk investments (bonds) and low-risk investments (cash). You may have heard the old adage, "The whole is greater than the sum of its parts." This is often true of a well-allocated portfolio that provides for both strong growth opportunities and conservative, protection measures.

What is particularly effective about asset allocation is that the three primary investment classes don't necessarily react the same way to the current economic environment. In other words, when stocks are down, bonds may be up, and vice versa. Likewise, other countries may provide ample growth opportunities during periods when the U.S. economy may stumble.

Hence, foreign securities—in addition to domestic holdings—should be considered when setting up your portfolio. Cash is always a good anchor, no matter the environment, but keep in mind that it lacks the ability to keep up with inflation over the long term.

The Case of the Broken Window

Here's an illustration of how asset allocation works. Say you have a beautiful bay window in your living room overlooking your large, perfectly landscaped front yard. Your next-door neighbor, on the other hand, has a large window of the same size in his living room, but his is divided up into 12 different sections by windowpanes.

Enter the 10-year-old boy across the street who wants nothing more than to play professional baseball when he grows up. He's got a staggering batting average and you are constantly finding baseballs on your front lawn. One day, little Timmy tattoos a line drive straight into your bay window, shattering it into a million pieces. That's what can happen to an all-stock portfolio when the equity market takes a dramatic downturn.

But let's say it's your neighbor who's the unlucky one. The baseball makes a beeline through his front window and lands on the Victorian sofa. However, your neighbor doesn't suffer nearly as much damage because the ball only broke one of twelve windowpanes; and one pane is a lot cheaper to replace than an entire bay window.

In portfolio terms, his window would have represented 12 different asset classes: Maybe he's got a combination of small-, mid-, and large-capitalization stocks, growth stocks, value stocks, international stocks, utility stocks, real estate holdings, government bonds, corporate bonds, CDs, and money market accounts. In other words, a decline in the stock market isn't going to tank his entire portfolio, and little Timmy won't have to work quite so many afternoon chores to pay for the windowpane replacement.

The Wisdom of Rebalancing

Because the markets rise and fall without any regard for your personal wishes, it's prudent every once in awhile to review and possibly "rebalance your portfolio." This means to sell off some of your holdings that have increased in price and, therefore, represent a larger part of your portfolio. You may find that your stock investments have raced forward while your bond investments have lagged behind, which throws your asset allocation out of whack.

At first glance, the new allocation may seem perfectly acceptable because, overall, your portfolio is performing well. However, what's really happened is that a larger portion of your portfolio has become far too risky.

A huge allocation to stocks may be fine if you're 25, but if you're 55 and worried about your money being there when you retire, you'll want to maintain a healthy balance among your securities selections.

This means selling off winners to buy some more lower-priced losers, and that may seem counterintuitive. It's not. Remember this mantra that describes how you make money by investing:

"Buy Low, Sell High."

Selling investments that have increased in price allows you to cash in on your good fortune. If you use this money to buy lower-priced investments, you are repositioning—or "rebalancing"—your portfolio to take advantage of future price increases.

If you have a 5- to 10-year time horizon before you need to access your money, your asset allocation will have the best chance to succeed. Over time, your portfolio will experience the ripples and waves of nearly every kind of economic cycle—giving each investment category a chance to shine.

For example, if stocks experience a long-term bull run, you may find that your portfolio has a higher percentage of stocks than you originally allocated. Unless your financial goals or personal situation has changed and now calls for a greater allocation of stocks, you should really rebalance your portfolio to get back to that original allocation between stocks, bonds, and cash.

Review your investments regularly, at least once a year, to see if you need to rebalance the portfolio.

On the other hand, you may need to reassess your original allocation if your personal circumstances change. Maybe you have to liquidate some of your portfolio for emergency cash, and find yourself falling behind in meeting your financial goals. In this case, you may need to increase your stock allocation to better position your portfolio for increased growth opportunities.

Or, as you grow older and approach retirement, you may wish to construct a more conservative portfolio in order to protect your investment earnings. This scenario may call for a lower allocation of stocks and an increase in bond and cash holdings.

Ideally, you shouldn't change your asset allocation based on market conditions but rather only when your own financial goals or circumstances change.

INVESTMENT OPTIONS

The Mutual Fund

Like most things, people learn about investing by taking baby steps. One of the early rungs on those steps are mutual funds, because they're easy to understand and can be one of the simplest and least expensive investment vehicles around. Perfect for the novice investor, but also a frequent choice of experienced investors seeking efficiency and diversification.

A mutual fund is composed of many different individual securities, all collected under one roof. And there are various different types of mutual funds, each consisting of security investments designed to meet a specific objective, be it long-term growth, immediate income, or to preserve money you already have.

Take a growth stock mutual fund for instance. It may own shares in IBM, Microsoft, General Motors, Philip Morris, and some other big name companies. It may also hold shares in some smaller but potentially lucrative companies that you've never heard of.

The advantage of a mutual fund is that you don't have to go out and buy shares in all of these companies yourself or research and figure out in which ones to invest. You just invest a little money, and so do a bunch of other people from places like Newberry, South Carolina, and Parsippany, New Jersey, and basically all over the country. But the great part is professional money managers manage this large pool of money, buying and selling stocks on behalf of all the mutual fund shareholders. These are the guys who follow the markets and figure out which are the most successful companies; they do the investing for you. They are not perfect—sometimes they make spectacular mistakes—but they know a whole lot more about the market than most of us.

When the money manager thinks a company's not doing so well, he or she will sell its shares and invest in something else. And the mutual fund company will let you know how you're doing, sending you a statement every quarter or so, as well as semiannual and annual reports and a yearly prospectus. The statement is like your bank statement, it tells you how much money your investment made or lost. It may look confusing at first, but just look for the line that reads "market value," and that's how much your investment is currently worth in dollar terms.

How to Pick a Mutual Fund

You can start your search online with some of the more common, household name fund families, like Fidelity and Vanguard. Read layperson-friendly magazines like *SmartMoney* to get additional ideas, then look them up online or talk to a financial advisor.

Boring as it may sound, one way you'll want to research a mutual fund is by reading its annual report and prospectus. Annual reports detail in which companies a mutual fund invests. When it comes to prospectuses, most of the stuff you need to know will be in the first four pages of the prospectus.

What you want to look for is whether or not the fund has been around awhile. It's not a great idea to invest in a fund less than five years old; ten years is better. Then check out how well it has made money for its investors, which is expressed as a percentage. Don't be too worried if the returns for one year or less aren't that great, or even negative. Any fund worth its weight in salt has down periods, which allows the money manager to buy more shares when prices are low. That's why checking out the long-term performance is more important than short-term numbers.

Next you want to check out how much the money manager charges each investor to run the fund. Anything from .02 to 2.00 percent of your investment is average. Don't necessarily shy away from a fund because it has a high fee; gauge the costs against the fund's performance. I don't mind paying more if the fund's always earning me money. I don't want to pay more if the fund doesn't have a consistent track record of making the bucks.

However, mutual funds tend to be quite similar in holdings, so if you're planning to invest in a plain-vanilla mutual fund like many others, there's no value to paying a higher fee—this will only reduce your return. Indexed funds typically offer the lowest fees, because they track the holdings of specific indexes and are not actively managed. The Vanguard Family of Funds (www.vanguard.com) has long held a reputation for low fund fees.

Every fund prospectus contains a handy chart that shows how much you pay in fees per $1,000 invested. It's a convenient doodad that eliminates having to break out your calculator and makes the fees look a little more palpable.

You'll also want to read the bio of the fund manager. You don't want some guy with less than 5 years in the business, although there are some good exceptions out there. However, 10 years or more experience is better.

Just so you know, you can definitely lose money investing in a mutual fund, and don't let anyone tell you otherwise. Even if you buy one in a bank, it is not guaranteed by the government or the FDIC or the SEC or the CIA or anybody else. Whether or not you make money or lose money depends solely on the performance of the mutual fund(s) you select.

There are "load" funds and "no-load" funds. A "load" is a sales commission—it goes straight to the advisor who's trying to sell you the fund. Do your comparative research on fund fees because sometimes you'll run across an advisor who sells only funds with the highest commissions. These are the advisors to avoid.

I know it seems like a lot of work, but you can find your own mutual fund by conducting research and buying directly from the fund company, thus avoiding have to pay a sales commission. You can read the fund's prospectus and decide which fund you want without having to pay a cent for advice.

The time to pay for investment advice is when you meet and develop a lifelong relationship with a fee-based financial advisor you can really trust. If you know he or she is truly looking out for your interests and is going to recommend investments that suit your individual needs—now and in the future—then it's okay to pay them an hourly fee for the time they spend educating and helping you make investment decisions. Relying on a professional investment advisor who knows the industry and works in it all day, every day, can help save a single parent from having to do all the work on your own.

Or, you can do the research and investing yourself. In doing so, you build your own knowledge. A company like Vanguard has lots of self-education materials on its Web site to help you make prudent decisions at the least cost. At very least, do lots of reading before you meet with an advisor so you have a basic understanding of what he or she is talking about, and take a list of questions with you.

There are a million investments out there. An investment in a mutual fund is one of the easiest you can make. If you start learning today, it gets a lot easier as time goes by. Pretty soon, you'll actually understand what the heck you're doing and have the confidence to learn about more complex types of investments.

But even if you go no further down the investing road than a mutual fund, you've done good. You may continue contributing and accumulating money toward your goals via this diversified investment vehicle.

Stocks

Stocks are shares you own in a company. If you are a stockholder, you own a proportionate share in the corporation's assets and you may be paid a share of the company's earnings in the form of dividends.

Over the course of investment history, stocks have proven to outperform every other type of investment over long periods of time. Stocks are considered to be a riskier investment than bonds or cash and their prices tend to fluctuate more sharply—both up and down—than other types of asset classes.

How to Choose a Stock

If you wish to buy individual stocks instead of a mutual fund, be sure to research the company before investing. You should understand its products or services, its market, as well as whether it has a sound balance sheet, cash-flow management, and competent directors and managers. You should also consider projected earnings estimates and the buy-neutral-sell views of recognized investment analysts. This type of information can be found online at a myriad of different financial Web sites, such as www.finance.yahoo.com.

Free Time =
Freedom from Mind-Numbing Discussions with Spouse

I have a theory about single parents and time management. It may feel like you never have any time, but it's actually a matter of energy. You do have time. You have time for yourself that married couples lack—nights after your children have gone to bed (or teenagers have moved past valuing your company). Consider using this free time wisely with the following suggestions:

1. *Exercise. Increase your energy level so you'll have more energy to accomplish everything two parents do in one day, only all by yourself. You can do aerobics, Pilates, free weights, and any number of other activities within the confines of your own home. Absolutely free. You can even do it while you zone out in front of the TV.*

2. *Cook. Prepare nutritious meals for the next day (or week). That way all you have to do is reheat when you get home from work. And with a little ingenuity, you may even be able to do this while you zone out in front of the TV.*

3. *Read. Research and read whatever stokes your interest, furthers your education, or moves you closer toward your long-term goals. Examples include putting in extra hours to help you get ahead in your career, learning principles of investing, how to do your taxes, or develop new streams of income. You need nothing more than a local library and/or Internet access and that illusionary free time (uniquely yours since you don't have to listen to your spouse's day at work or problems with foot fungus).*

An additional bonus is that your increased knowledge equals power out there in the real world. But in your world, knowledge can lead to increased self-confidence. Recognize that as a single parent, you do have free time. Use it wisely; appreciate the silence.

More about Stocks

There are about a gazillion stocks out there in which to invest (or at least it seems that way), whether you're stock picking yourself or leaving it up to a money manager. The following are a few extra tidbits to help you understand what is available.

Value Stocks

Studies have proven that over a long-term investment horizon, a value-oriented investment strategy will outperform a growth-oriented investment strategy. This is great news for women who tend to invest more conservatively, hold securities for a long time, and most significantly, understand the value of getting a great product for a low price.

Bargain shopping is at the heart of the value strategy, which is basically buying stocks with prices that are actually lower than the company's current value. This can happen because of poor quarterly earnings or if the company is embroiled in legal battles, or perhaps it's just plain being ignored by the market in favor of more flashy alternatives.

The key to value investing is finding undervalued stocks that the rest of the market has overlooked for one reason or another. Shelby M. C. Davis, a noted value mutual fund money manager, once said, "Just like I don't judge a child with every report card, I don't disown companies when they have a bad quarter." As a parent, perhaps you can see his point.

The following are a few tips if you want to try your hand at value stock picking:

- Buy at a price you can live with for awhile
- Favor companies that buy back their stock
- Minimize risk by buying stocks that have already been bruised
- Look for the potential for positive change
- Add to your position during price declines (remember, "Buy Low, Sell High")
- Sell your position gradually

Growth Stocks

Growth stocks, on the other hand, are the darlings of the market. Their earnings and/or share prices are considered on the rise, so it's best to get in on the ground floor and enjoy the ride for the long term. The problem with growth stocks is that they tend to be quite popular. Once the buying frenzy is initiated, prices may become inflated to the point where the stock is priced higher than it is actually worth. That's a precarious position. On the other hand, if you managed to buy in early and sell during the market frenzy that inflates price, it can also be quite lucrative.

The following are a few tips if you want to try your hand at growth stock picking:

- Choose companies with increasing demand for their products or services
- Choose companies with groundbreaking products
- Choose companies with past success breaking into new markets
- Choose companies that are undisputed leaders in their respective industries

Top Down, Bottom Up

This is not a reference to swigging beer in the back seat of a convertible. In fact, it's just investment hoo-hah for a couple of rather simple stock selection strategies. "Top Down" means that the money manager looks at the overall health and well-being of a particular sector, industry, or country. For example, let's say he or she believes that large company stocks are in pretty good shape. The economy is strong, consumers have plenty of disposable income, and established businesses are growing at a controlled clip.

Does this mean all large companies would make good investments? No, it's just a strong trend. So the next thing the manager does is look down at the next level to see what specific industries are poised for profits, such as telecommunications or pharmaceutical companies. Within the sector, he narrows his choices down to the individual companies. In a sense, he started at the top of the category and combed his way down.

This also works within particular industries, such as information technology. A manager may believe it is poised to do well over the next 5–10 years, so he begins seeking out any and all companies that stand to increase earnings. His research may span small, midsized, or large companies, both domestic and international.

The same goes with foreign stocks. First he picks a country he likes, then he pares down to specific sectors and industries to, finally, the individual companies he anticipates will produce strong returns. He starts at the top and works his way down to individual holdings.

"Bottom Up" is just the opposite. Some money managers aren't primarily concerned with the market trends of a specific industry or country.

They find companies they think are good investments. They check out the books and interview managers, customers, suppliers, etc., until completely convinced that the company will provide strong returns for shareholders.

Then, and only then, do they take off the blinders and look at peripheral factors. Whether competitors in the same industry are also poised for success, if other similar sized businesses are taking off, if the country where the business is headquartered is viable or on the edge of collapse.

In short, they start at the bottom and work their way up to examine trends that have propelled this company to be a good investment. This allows them to spot other companies that may be in just as good of shape.

Neither the top-down nor the bottom-up strategy is absolute, and there are a lot of money managers who fall somewhere in between. Top down and bottom up are simply starting points to begin research. Ultimately, all factors should be considered when choosing a stock.

Global Consumer, Global Investor

Perhaps you're a soccer mom who drives a Honda Odyssey or Toyota Sienna minivan. Or perhaps you're a music or movie aficionado who insists on buying only Sony, Samsung, or Panasonic when it comes to electronics. But even if you "go international" only by frequenting Italian, Mexican, or Chinese restaurants, you're a global consumer.

It's not surprising that in many industries, foreign competitors have bested the United States when it comes to consumer products. Just look around your house. Pick up some cheesy bric-a-brac your in-laws brought back from their last vacation to Disneyland. It was probably made in China. It seems like most everything is made in China these days.

There's the key. As a global consumer, you are already a global investor, because you are entrusting your money to a foreign company. In exchange, you expect good performance of the product you've bought. For this reason, investing your money in foreign companies is not considered as risky as it used to be.

If there's a quality foreign product you admire, there's a good chance the company that makes it is just as worthy, so why not place that same faith in your investment portfolio? In fact, studies have shown that investment portfolios with the least amount of risk were those with at least some exposure to overseas markets as opposed to an all-U.S. stock portfolio.

So not only does investing globally offer you the chance to invest in the growth companies whose products you frequently purchase, but buying foreign holdings also helps reduce the overall risk of your investment portfolio.

The easiest way to invest globally is through a mutual fund, which will research and purchase a large number of stocks and/or bonds to further reduce your risk. There are even mutual funds that specialize exclusively in foreign holdings. These are called "International Funds."

Mutual funds that combine foreign and U.S. investments are called "Global Funds."

A Safe(r) Way to Invest in Real Estate

Maybe you can't afford to invest in real estate to secure rental income, but it is possible to become something similar to landlord, only free of property management responsibilities.

A Real Estate Investment Trust (REIT) is a mutual fund that invests primarily in real estate holdings, allowing you to make a small single investment and benefit from both diversification and professional management. Not only do REITs allow the smaller investor to participate in large-scale commercial projects, but they are required to pay out high dividends.

Another advantage is that REITs are considered relatively less risky than many stocks. This is because REITs have the ability to appreciate in value during periods of both inflation and economic strength due to their underlying property values, occupancy levels, and rental rates—which may rise no matter what the rest of the investment market is doing.

REIT shares can be purchased on the major stock exchanges or through a stockbroker, or you can buy REIT shares in a real estate sector mutual fund.

Bonds

Corporations, governments, and municipalities issue bonds to raise money to reinvest in the organization or fund government services, like schools, roads, and bridges. In return, bonds typically pay the investor a fixed interest rate. In this way, a bond is like a loan you make to a company, and the company pays you back over time, with interest.

Bonds are considered fixed income investments that provide a regular income stream and can help diversify a portfolio. Most bonds pay out periodic interest and return your principal at maturity—which is to say at the end of the loan term.

Interest rates may be the most significant factor that impacts a bond's value. When interest rates fall, the value of existing bonds rises because their fixed interest rates are more attractive in the market than the lower rates for new issues. Similarly, when interest rates rise, the value of existing bonds with lower, fixed interest rates tends to fall.

Economic conditions may also cause bond values, particularly corporate bonds, to fluctuate. An economic change that adversely affects a company's business may reduce the company's ability to make interest or principal payments on issued bonds.

The most important factor influencing the bond market is the country's current state of inflation. Higher inflation reduces the future buying power of the fixed interest payments that bond investors receive, so bonds are not all that popular an investment during a high inflation period.

On the other hand, economic factors that indicate lower inflation, such as higher unemployment or weak gross domestic product (GDP) growth, are welcome news to bond investors. In this scenario, bond prices tend to rise and bond investors can get a better return by selling their investments.

How to Choose a Bond

Here are some factors to consider when choosing a bond or bond fund:

- Compare ratings—look for a high-quality rating from industry analysts Moody's or Standard & Poor's, which reflect the issuing company's stability and level of risk;
- Interest rate—the rate you're offered at issuance may fluctuate under various market conditions based on the bond's fluctuating price, but you're assured full payment if you hold the bond to maturity
- Call ability—some bond issuers maintain the right to recall the bond before maturity, but they often offer a higher interest rate in return for this right
- Duration—how long you must own the bond before it reaches maturity; the lower the duration of the bond, the less volatile it will be

Buying bonds contributes more to the American economy than do stocks. When you buy a stock, you're seeking profits for just you and the company you're investing in. However, when you buy a state or municipal bond, you're providing needed capital to build housing, schools, parks, roads, infrastructure, and hospitals, thereby creating a greater universe for new jobs.

State and municipal bonds also lower the taxpayer's burden when it comes to financing these projects, so they in turn offer tax-free yields. Obviously, there are a lot of advantages to buying bonds—both personal and public—so it's important to understand how they work and the most advantageous ways to use bonds within your investment portfolio.

Ladder Bonds

One strategy that will help your bond portfolio in any interest rate environment is to "ladder" their maturities. Diversifying fixed income assets among a combination of short-, intermediate-, and long-term bond maturities allows you to access your money, or at least reevaluate your investment options in light of interest rates, every few years.

For example, say you buy a 1-year, a 3-year, and a 7-year bond. After the first year, you may roll your 1-year bond over to another 1-year bond, or buy a longer-term maturity, depending on what rates are doing. Two years later, you have the same choices regarding your 3-year bond, and in four more years, you may consider what to do with your 7-year maturity bond. Instead of getting locked into a particular interest rate environment, you have plenty of options to change the course of your bond investments as time wears on.

Bonds may lack the stellar performance potential of stocks, but they offer stability and diversification during inevitable economic downswings. Bonds generally offer a relatively safe, predictable income stream that you can count on even when your stock portfolio has taken a hit.

By laddering bond investments, you will always have cash options, and you never have to get stuck with a low-yield portfolio when rates are up, or vice versa. This strategy is particularly advantageous to investors who rely on yields from fixed income investments to pay for regular, household living expenses.

Money Market Accounts and Certificates of Deposit

A money market account is a deposit account at a bank that sort of blends the advantages of a checking and savings account. Like a savings account, you receive a relatively high interest rate on your deposit. In addition, you have checking and debit privileges that are subject to limits.

A certificate of deposit, better known as a "CD," is also offered by a banking institution and is federally insured by the FDIC (limits apply). CDs are offered with a fixed term that can range anywhere from three months to five years along with a fixed interest rate. The CD is designed to be held, intact, until the end of the maturity term, at which point the money may be withdrawn along with the accrued interest. CDs tend to offer relatively higher rates of interest than deposit accounts from which you may make withdrawals.

Autumn is the season when many CDs mature, and investors start looking around for higher rate products in which to roll over their CD money. One overlooked area you might want to consider is what they call "brokered CDs."

Brokered CDs are generally sold off to raise capital for smaller issuing banks. They tend to be offered at higher interest rates than most, and offer the added advantage of a broker shopping for the best rates on your behalf.

Another benefit to brokered CDs is that many of the selling brokerages will provide additional guaranteed coverage beyond the standard $100,000 to $250,000 FDIC coverage. This additional guarantee allows investors who hold multiple CDs at several different banks to consolidate their investments and still be covered. Otherwise, your CD assets may not be covered if you exceed the FDIC maximum guarantee per institution.

The following are two CD strategies you may want to consider:

- S&P 500 Indexed CDs allow you to participate in stock market returns while preserving principal.
- Purchasing brokered CDs of various maturities allows you to ladder them and shop for higher rates at shorter intervals.

A Word about Market Risk

What's ironic about market risk is that the factors that cause it often have little to do with your particular investments. Rather, worldwide events can trigger downturns that reduce the value of your holdings. Consider the impact of 9/11 and the global reach of the subprime mortgage debacle.

That's why the best way to combat market risk is simply to diversify your investments across different types of asset classes. This technique helps reduce the risk posed by investing all of your assets in one source and helps offset temporary losses of some portfolio holdings via the strong performance of others.

Diversification is particularly important when it comes to retirement planning. Many people feel that because they are participating in their company pension or stock purchase plan, their retirement needs are covered. However, it's wise to balance dependence upon your company's financial health with various personal investments as well.

Otherwise, you could end up like many Enron employees in 2002. When the company went under, not only did they lose their job, they lost their pensions and assets invested in company stock via their 401(k) and employee stock ownership plans.

Remember the 10-year-old baseball player and the case of the broken window: Don't place your income-earning ability and all of your investment prospects in the hands of one company. Diversify. Diversify. Diversify.

College Investment Plans and Resources

The difference in the average lifetime earnings between a college and high school graduate is nearly $1 million. So sure, we all know that in the long run, college pays for itself. But what matters for a single parent is who pays for it now.

Fortunately, where financial aid is concerned, this is one of the advantages to being a single parent. With one parent, one income, and one or more children—the key is to look on paper as poor as humanly possible. On paper, at least, this usually isn't much of a stretch for single parents.

When your student begins to apply for college admission, that's the time to complete the "Free Application for Federal Student Aid," more commonly known as the FAFSA (www.fafsa.ed.gov). This is a universal application for financial aid, no matter what college your child ends up attending (note that some schools may require additional forms). Once you complete and submit the form, this government agency will calculate an Expected Family Contribution (EFC) based on yours and your student's combined financial picture.

This information will be sent to both you and any colleges your student is considering attending (which he or she indicates on the form). Then, each individual college determines how much financial aid will be offered to your child if he or she attends that school, and in what form it shall take.

Your student must resubmit the FAFSA every year. This is easy to do if you register for an account online (www.fafsa.ed.gov), as you can store your form online and simply update it each year. Some of the key points to completing the FAFSA include:

- Read the instructions carefully—this may seem obvious, but the FAFSA is a little trickier in that sometimes it asks for parental information, and other times questions refer exclusively to the student.

- Apply early—the FAFSA has a deadline, but you should apply well before then because schools start doling out their money and may run low by the time they receive late entries.

- Complete your tax return before you apply for the FAFSA—so many questions will be easy to answer if you do. You don't have to actually file your return before you submit the FAFSA, but it's good to complete it so you include all the correct information on your form.

- The information on your FAFSA must match what you file on your tax return. Schools may request a copy of your filed tax return to verify information before they will determine your student's financial awards.

Financial Aid Stigma

There's something you should know about financial aid. Even households making a six-figure income can qualify for financial aid. Colleges encourage every prospective student, regardless of his or her socioeconomic background, to apply for financial aid with a FAFSA.

So, you don't need to feel like you are the lone, lowly single parent who didn't save enough to pay for your child to go to college.

In fact, it would appear that since so many students receive financial aid these days, colleges actually establish their pricing based on the fact that most students will receive additional funding for college expenses. It's like they price on a curve or a handicap. How else would you account for tuition increases, on average, of 8 percent per year?

Over the last decade, college tuition has been growing at four times the overall inflation rate each year, which is more inflated than gasoline or health care. Funny that salaries haven't increased by quite the same margin.

This is an extremely important point to discuss with your student when deciding where to attend college. Why? Because you need to weigh the cost of sending her to college against the subsequent job opportunities available to her once she graduates.

For example, if an out-of-state school has the same programs of study and shares a similar reputation to that of an in-state school, it's only logical to send your child in state. If it appears unlikely—and you need to work to get your child to understand this—that the school that costs $20,000 more a year will yield a significantly higher salary job, then it just doesn't make sense to spend the extra money (or incur the additional debt).

No matter how great a school's reputation is for tailgate parties and Greek life.

After all, a school isn't academically better just because it's not located in your state; but its tuition will be higher simply because it's located in another state. A general rule of thumb is to examine the in-state tuitions of various schools to help your child select comparable in-state schools to his out-of-state preferences.

You have to go with what you can afford. Children have the ability to make friends wherever they go (or need to practice this skill); and all will work out even if you don't send your child to his or her irrationally priced first choice.

This may not always be true, but you can rest assured that should your child have a tough time adjusting to life at college, the reasons have nothing to do with the amount of the tuition you pay. You can't buy happiness, but you can find a good college education at an afford-able price.

Grants and Loans

College scholarships, fellowships, and grants are basically gifts that do not require repayment. Loans, on the other hand, require funds to be repaid in full with interest.

The Federal Pell Grant is probably the best-known grant that helps undergraduates pay for their education. The grant depends on the amount of the EFC toward education expenses and whether the student plans to attend college full- or part-time. As long as a grant is used for qualified college expenses by the student, grant money is not taxed and does not have to be repaid.

The Federal Stafford Loan, Federal Perkins, and PLUS Loans offer low interest rates to cover college expenses. Interest rates on these loans tend to be lower than those on other types of loans or credit vehicles, and do not have to be paid off until about six months after the student graduates from college (assuming continuous attendance).

- Federal Perkins Loans are offered by participating schools to students who demonstrate the greatest financial need (Federal Pell Grant recipients get top priority).
- Federal Stafford Loans are extended to graduate and undergraduate students who demonstrate financial need.
- Both Perkins and Stafford loans require students to apply and agree to the loan repayment.
- PLUS Loans are offered to parents, who must have a reasonably good credit score and meet other criteria to qualify.

College Fund Investments

Traditionally, popular vehicles for growing a college fund included stocks, bonds, and mutual funds. All good choices, but now there are even better, tax-advantaged alternatives designed to encourage saving money for college. These include:

- 529 Prepaid tuition plans—you paid a locked-in tuition rate today that is invested to grow at the same rate as tuition costs, so when your child enters college, his or her tuition will be covered;

- 529 College savings plans—invested in mutual funds; state tax deductions on contributions; earnings used for college expenses grow tax-free;
- Coverdell Education Savings Account (ESA)—maximum annual contributions of $2,000 are tax deductible and earnings grow tax-free;
- Education Savings Bond Program—special purpose municipal zero-coupon bonds that offer discounts on college tuition if your child attends an in-state school.

529 Prepaid Tuition Plan

Prepaid tuition plans allow you to pay for your child's college tuition at today's rates, even though he or she won't be attending college for years in the future when tuition rates have increased substantially. In other words, you can lock in today's tuition rate either with a lump sum or a payment plan, regardless of when your child attends.

The program will then pay the future college tuition of the beneficiary at any of the state's public colleges. In most cases, you can use the plan proceeds to pay for qualified college expenses at private or out-of-state institutions, but each state's plan differs. This is something you should check into so that you don't have to decide where your child will attend college while he or she's still a toddler.

Guidelines (plan criteria vary by state):

- You or the student beneficiary must be a resident of the state at the time you open an account.
- Most prepaid plans require you to open an account at least three years prior to using it to pay for higher education.
- Students are typically required to be 15 years old or younger when the account is opened.
- Anyone (grandparents, godparents, etc.) may contribute to the prepaid plan.
- If your child receives a scholarship, plan proceeds may be used for any qualified expenses not covered by the scholarship, or you can assign benefits to another child coming up the pike, or you can obtain a refund (state plans vary on how this is handled).
- The same applies if your child does not attend college.
- Just because you prepay for college, there's no guarantee your child will get into one.

529 College Savings Plan

Every state in the United States (as well as Washington, D.C.) offers a 529 college savings plan. You don't have to choose the plan offered by your state, but in many states your contributions are deductible from your state income tax return, so it's a good option to consider.

Unlike the prepaid account, your money is invested for growth and managed by professional money managers. Typically you select an investment option based on how long until your child reaches college age. The longer the time frame, the more aggressively your money will be invested. As your child grows older and closer to college age, your investment is typically transferred to a more conservative portfolio to better preserve the assets accumulated.

But make no mistake: The 529 college savings plan is an investment (not a guaranteed prepaid plan), and you can lose money with it just like any other investment plan. Also, state plans tend to have limited investment options as compared to selecting and managing your own stock or mutual fund portfolio.

Guidelines (plan criteria vary by state):

- 529s pose no age, state, or income restrictions to open an account.
- Most plans allow you to open an account for as little as $25 or $50, with the same amount as a subsequent monthly contribution (some plans allow as little as $15 a month).
- You may contribute any amount a year, with a lifetime maximum of $250,000 or more.
- You do not have to pay federal taxes on withdrawals made for qualified higher education expenses.
- Many state plans also waive taxes on qualified withdrawals.
- Many states offer additional advantages to residents, such as a state tax deduction, a matching grant, scholarship opportunities, protection from creditors, and exemption from state financial aid calculations.
- Beneficiaries may be of any age, and you can rename the beneficiary or tap the account penalty-free if your child receives a scholarship.
- 529 plans are given favorable treatment when applying for financial aid; the balance is multiplied by 5.64 percent, and eligibility is decreased by only that margin (e.g., $15,000 \times 5.64\% = \$846$; only $846 is considered for financial aid purposes).

- The account is good for up to 10 years past the beneficiary's high school graduation.
- You may open up a 529 for yourself to pursue a higher education degree.
- You may reassign yourself as the beneficiary and use any leftover money to attend college classes during retirement.

Distributions not used for qualified college expenses (tuition, room, board, books, supplies, and computer equipment) will be taxed and may also get hit with a 10 percent penalty when withdrawn. However, this is only true of the earnings, not your original contribution amounts.

If your child earns a full scholarship, you may change the beneficiary or withdraw money and only pay the taxes on earnings (the 10% penalty won't apply). However, you may use the fund money for any qualified expenses not covered by the scholarship. If your child simply doesn't go to college, you may withdraw the money and pay taxes and the 10 percent penalty on any interest earned.

Whoever opens the account—whether it's you, grandparents, or anyone else—owns the account. The student beneficiary cannot withdraw money to use as he or she pleases. Also, even if you open the account, anyone may contribute to it. States vary as to whom can claim tax advantages for contributions made.

You may open both a 529 savings plan and state prepaid tuition plan and get state tax deductions for both. The savings plan may also be used in conjunction with Hope and Lifetime Learning tax credits and the Education Savings Account. Visit www.collegesavings.org for more information.

Coverdell Education Savings Account

Formerly known as the Education IRA, this savings account allows you to choose your own investments instead of from a limited choice of age-oriented portfolios, as with a 529 savings plan. You may open one with a mutual fund company or brokerage firm.

Guidelines:

- You may contribute only up to $2,000 per year, per student.
- Earnings are tax deferred and, if used for qualified college expenses, tax-free when withdrawn.
- There is no tax deduction for contributions.

HEAD OF HOUSEHOLD TIP: SAVE FOR COLLEGE WHILE BUYING FOR YOUR FAMILY

Open an account and register your debit and credit cards at www.upromise.com. This is a unique program that has struck up a deal with literally thousands of retail stores and restaurants that you visit every day. Every time you use one of your registered cards with one of these participating vendors, a percentage of your purchase will be contributed to your college savings account. You can link your 529 savings plan to your Upromise account and the savings will be deposited quarterly, and you can check your Upromise contributions online. You can save anywhere from 1 to 10 percent of your purchase price, depending on the vendor, and they run additional promotions all the time. The earlier you start, the more savings you reap. It's free money contributed to your account based on purchases that you're going to make anyway.

- You may use withdrawals for private elementary and high school expenses as well as college.
- There are income restrictions and phaseouts for opening an ESA, but they are pretty liberal (head of household tax filers may earn up to $95,000 a year to make the maximum contribution).

Education Savings Bond Program

If you own a series I U.S. Bond or a series EE Bond purchased after 1989, you may be able to cash in these bonds and not have to pay taxes on interest earned that you use to pay for qualified college expenses. There is an income limitation (around $80,000 for head of household) indexed each year.

Using Personal Resources to Fund College

Looking for other college funding ideas? Look around you. If you're sitting peacefully in a home you own, you may have an asset you can tap for college funds. While a home equity loan does charge interest, interest rates tend to be lower than other personal credit sources and the interest you pay each year is tax deductible, just like your first mortgage.

Many 401(k) plans allow employees to borrow from their 401(k) accounts for major expenses, such as a home or a child's college education. The money you borrow must be repaid with interest—but all payments (including the interest) go back into your account. Payments will come directly out of your paycheck and keep in mind that if you quit your job before you pay the loan back, all monies will be due right away or you'll have to pay income taxes on the outstanding amount.

You may withdraw from any type of IRA to pay for qualifying education expenses without incurring the usual 10 percent penalty for premature withdrawals before age 59½ (although income taxes may still be assessed).

However, complete a FAFSA and tap the financial aid opportunities available to your student before depleting your personal resources. Most financial experts favor student loans over tapping your 401(k) or home equity—reasoning that a young adult would rather pay off a student loan herself than have her impoverished parent come live with her.

In a nutshell, protect yourself and your future. An affordable college education is available to everyone, and your children have a lot longer time period than you do to pay off loans.

RETIREMENT INVESTMENT PLANS

The 401(k), 457, and 403(b) Plans

- 401(k)—Sponsored by private sector employers
- 457—Sponsored by government agency employers
- 403(b)—Sponsored by educational institute and nonprofit employers

The 401(k), 403(b), and 457 are investment programs that many employers now offer to help employees save and invest money for retirement. To participate, your employer will take money out of your paycheck before you even receive it and invest it in your 401(k) (or similar) account. This may in fact seem like the last thing you need—what, with those payments on your new HDTV.

Single parents in particular may feel like they can't worry about retirement when they're living paycheck to paycheck. But listen: even if there is a Social Security program when you retire, it was never designed to cover all of your living expenses. Social Security benefits currently only provide about a quarter of what recipients need for housing, food, insurance, and other expenses in retirement. And by the time you retire, benefits may be reduced to an even lower percentage. That means you're going to have to come up with all the rest of the dough—and that's after you stop earning income.

That's where 401(k) plans (and the like) come in. Sure, they take money out of your paycheck. But it's still your money. It goes into an account where it grows for years and years until it blossoms into this beautiful nest egg ready to be tapped when you retire. Well, ideally. You'll get a statement every quarter that tells you how much your 401(k) account has grown, and you'll say, "Wow, I actually have a net worth" (instead of a net deficit).

As long as you keep contributing, your account may continue to grow even if its investments aren't exactly racing along. When markets start tanking, many people consider stopping their investment contributions. Don't do this. Why?

"Buy Low, Sell High."

When you contribute money to your 401(k) during a down market, your money buys more. It's like going shopping during a sale where you can pick up great products for cheap prices.

But buying a bargain in the investment world can give you a return in the future. Buy low, and when the stock prices eventually increase, you can sell for a profit. It's like buying an expensive sweater for the bargain price of $30, then reselling it a few years later for $100. And nobody cares that it's used.

There are additional perks to investing in a 401(k) plan. For some, not all, contributing to your 401(k) can actually allow you to bring home more money each paycheck. If you're at one of those thresholds where you make just enough to tip you into another tax bracket, your 401(k) contributions can take you back down into the lower bracket. That's because they take out the investment contribution before they figure how much you owe in taxes. As your income in each paycheck shrinks, so do the taxes they take out. Lo and behold, you could end up bringing home a few more bucks than you did previously, even having dropped a percentage of your gross income into the 401(k) account.

Here's the real kicker. A lot of companies will match your contribution up to a certain percentage. Usually it's around .50 for each dollar and up to about 4 percent of your contribution (or more).

For example, if 2 percent of your gross paycheck (the total amount before taxes and stuff are taken out) is $30.00, then the company match would add another $15.00 at 50¢ for each dollar. That's just plain free money! And voila! You're sinking $45.00 a paycheck, or $90.00 a month, into your 401(k) retirement investment account. That's over $1,000.00 a year, before any investment earnings.

Best of all, you're only letting go a nominal amount per paycheck, and let's face it, that's just one less night you take the family out to dinner. Plus, the fewer taxes paid will at least in part offset the take-home loss.

Of course, the government places a cap on how much you can invest in your 401(k) each year so that rich folks don't go hog wild with the tax shelter. In 2009, your total contribution must be less than $16,500. Once you reach age 50, you can make an additional "catch-up" contribution of $5,500 a year.

Be sure to keep ratcheting up your contribution amount to a higher percentage of your income—aim for at least a 1 percent increase each year if you start small. Ideally you want to get to the point where you "max out" your contribution limit without feeling the hit to your budget. But think about it. It's so much nicer to use the phrase "max out" in reference to an investment contribution rather than a credit card limit.

If you need your money, you can always get it. If you're under age 59½ and you just want to withdraw 401(k) money for your son's snowboard, it's really not worth it. You're going to get hit with the double whammy of income taxes on the amount you withdraw as well as a 10 percent federal penalty for early withdrawals (meaning, there's no way you need a snowboard if you're over 60).

Remember, these accounts are set up specifically to help you save for retirement, so they don't make it easy to tap your money.

However, a lot of companies will let you borrow up to half of your account balance for really legitimate expenses, such as buying a house, paying for your child's college, or if you get laid up with excessive medical bills. What's really cool is that while you have to pay your loan back with interest, all that money goes back into your account. They are going to take these payments out of your paycheck, but this time after taxes have been taken out. So then you're really going to feel it. However, if you feel it in your nice new home with your child in college and your medical bills paid, it won't feel quite so bad.

Leave your job? Lots of companies just let you leave your money in the 401(k) plan, although both of you stop contributing to it. Or, you can roll it over into a new IRA account. Also, plenty of companies will let you transfer your previous plan money into their 401(k), as soon as you qualify. Don't worry. You never lose this money; your old employer can't keep it.

There is one antiquated tactic called "vesting," in which your employer won't let you access the company contributions in your 401(k) account until a certain amount of time has passed. Vesting often happens in stages, where the money is 50 percent vested after a year or two, and 100 percent vested after a longer period.

However, in recent years—in light of the trend to change jobs more often—vesting periods have become much shorter and many employers have eliminated them altogether.

Regardless, a 401(k) plan (or the like) is still the absolute best plan for starting a retirement nest egg program. After that, you can do mutual funds or IRAs or annuities or whatever else. But start with your retirement plan at work.

The IRA

The IRA stands for "Independent Retirement Arrangement," and it's another vehicle designed for you to invest money intended to grow for retirement. There are two kinds of IRAs, the traditional version and the Roth version.

The main difference between the two has to do with when you pay taxes on the money you contribute and earn within the account.

- Traditional—you can deduct your annual contribution (subject to limitations) from your tax return, which will reduce your current income taxes. Your money may earn interest until you retire, at which time you may withdraw money and pay taxes on the interest you earned.

- Roth—you do not get a tax deduction on your annual contributions, but as long as you hold the account for at least five years and make withdrawals after age 59½, you don't have to pay any taxes on the interest earned in the account.

The amount you may contribute to an IRA or combination of IRAs each year is much lower than an employer-sponsored retirement plan ($5,000 in 2009; $6,000 for account owners age 50+), which is one of the reasons why it's best to max out your company plan first. However, if you still have money to contribute, the IRA is another good option for retirement savings with tax advantages.

The Traditional IRA

If you participate in a company retirement plan, there may be limits to the IRA contribution amount that you can deduct from your taxes. The deduction phases out based on your filing status and amount you earn. If you earn more than $63,000 (head of household; 2009), you won't be able to take any tax deduction at all, but you can still contribute to a traditional IRA.

The following are a few additional things you should know about a traditional IRA:

- It is an investment in a securities market, so it's possible to lose money on your investment.
- However, an IRA is a long-term investment, so the longer you own it, the lower the chances of losing money.
- If you make a withdrawal before age 59½, the money may be subject to a 10 percent early withdrawal penalty, in addition to income taxes.
- Investors may tap their IRA account penalty-free for certain qualified expenses, including a first home purchase, college expenses, medical bills, and health insurance premiums (although income taxes will still be owed).
- You must stop contributing and begin taking required minimum distributions (RMD) from your IRA beginning at age 70½.

The Roth IRA

The Roth makes an ideal complement to a 401(k) investment. If you earn more than $53,000, you may not deduct your contribution from a traditional IRA anyway, so you might as well open a Roth IRA instead. Roth IRA contributions are not tax deductible, but interest earned may be withdrawn tax-free after five years for qualified expenses or after age 59½.

You may contribute to a Roth IRA if you have taxable income and your modified adjusted gross income (AGI) is less than $120,000 (head of household; 2009). If you earn more than that, you may not contribute to a Roth.

After you've owned your Roth IRA account for five years or more, you may take out money without having to pay an early withdrawal penalty for qualified expenses such as a first-time home purchase, medical expenses, health insurance premiums, or if you become disabled.

The Roth is designed to accommodate today's longer-working pre-retirees. You may continue contributing earned income even after age 70½, and you don't have to make any RMD until you're ready.

The most important thing to remember about a Roth is that at the distribution end, you don't have to pay taxes. Here's why this is important.

The Social Security Administration reports that by 2018 the program will begin paying more in benefits than it collects in taxes and by 2041 the trust funds will be exhausted. You shouldn't worry too much about this, because the government will come up with a way to supplement the fund by then.

The part you do need to worry about is how the government will come up with the funds. It will likely raise taxes. It has never made sense to me that you work all your life and pay taxes toward Social Security so that you may receive benefits when you retire—and then you get taxed on those benefits too. But you do.

So when you retire and start receiving Social Security benefits, you're going to have to pay taxes on that money, and those taxes may be significantly higher than they are now because you're helping to pay for everyone else's retirement benefits.

If you have some other retirement accounts, like a traditional IRA and a 401(k) plan, you'll be paying taxes on the income you receive from those as well.

But with a Roth, you already paid taxes on your contributions and your interest earnings are tax-free. So with a Roth, you aren't going to have to pay those higher taxes when you're in retirement and making no income.

That's why the Roth is such a big deal. It's a complement to other income resources to help reduce your tax burden during retirement.

Real Estate in Your IRA

It may have never occurred to you, but you can actually invest in a piece of real estate as part of your IRA. This will allow the property to appreciate tax-deferred until you're ready to retire, but keep in mind that it's a tricky process that may require some professional expertise.

Basically, what's most important is that you must use already invested money from your IRA to make both the down payment and the ongoing mortgage payments on the property. Not only does real estate add a diversified dimension to a retirement portfolio, but you may enjoy the profits of the investment at a lower tax rate once you've retired and are past age 59½ (to avoid a 10% early withdrawal penalty).

There is one caution to keep in mind, however. Be aware of how this investment will affect your beneficiaries should you pass on before distributions. Many times heirs get stuck with neglected property and a mortgage burden in which the property will not pay for itself. Make sure you consider this option carefully and continue to evaluate its viability as part of your portfolio on a regular basis.

Like I said, tricky stuff, so get help from a financial advisor on how to structure your IRA if you think you'd like to use this money to make an investment in real estate.

The Annuity

An annuity combines the advantages of two worlds: investing and insurance. It is actually a legally binding contract you purchase from an insurance company, and with that contract comes certain guarantees, such as fixed rate account options, a death benefit payment, and even guaranteed income for life.

Just like 401(k) plans and IRAs, annuities are subject to a 10 percent penalty tax on withdrawals made before age 59½. Annuities also tend to charge higher administrative fees than other types of investments, such as mutual funds, which help fund the guarantees offered. Most annuities also impose "surrender charges" on any withdrawals made during the early years of the contract, which is basically a penalty fee (usually a percentage of the withdrawal made). Surrender fees typically reduce each year you own the contract and disappear altogether after about the fifth or seventh year.

Contributions to an annuity are not tax deductible unless you buy it under the umbrella of an IRA arrangement. There's usually not a big advantage to doing this, especially since the IRA umbrella mandates a $5,000 limit (2009) on contributions. Outside of an IRA, you can contribute pretty much as much as you want each year.

If you're not eligible to participate in a company 401(k) plan or have maxed out your contribution limits, an annuity offers an attractive investment alternative. The main advantage is that all earnings appreciate tax-deferred until you withdraw your money, which is ideally when you're retired and in a lower tax bracket.

The Fixed Annuity

The fixed annuity guarantees a fixed interest rate over a certain period of time. Returns may seem a little lackluster during a strong investment market, but during down periods, even a small gain can give you peace of mind.

The Variable Annuity

A variable annuity contract invests in various stock, bond, and cash mutual funds, also known as "portfolios" or "sub-accounts." All of the investment options are managed by professional money managers who oversee the day-to-day research and analysis for their assigned portfolios, and there are generally no limits to annual contributions.

Variable annuities are designed to build retirement income. They are subject to the same market risk as mutual funds and other securities, and you can most certainly lose money. However, should you die before you begin receiving annuity payments for retirement income, your beneficiaries are typically guaranteed to receive at least as much as your original investment, minus any withdrawals you've made.

It used to be that to receive this guaranteed income for life, you had to "annuitize" your contract. This means you relinquish all the money in your account to the insurance company in trade for guaranteed income for life. They have actuarial criteria to determine exactly how much guaranteed income you'll receive based on your life expectancy at the age you annuitize and how much money is in the account at that time.

That can be a pretty heady trade-off. In other words, if sometime after you make this trade-off you need additional money for an emergency, you can't pull it out of your annuity. A deal's a deal. As I said, it's a legally binding contract that you purchase.

However, in recent years, companies have loosened up this trade-off by offering income riders—for an additional fee—that will guarantee you a certain amount of income (usually a percentage of your account balance) for a certain period of time or the rest of your life, and yet you can still tap the account for additional withdrawals if you need to.

These riders come with limitations though, ranging from how much additional money you can withdraw at a time to what investments you're allowed to choose. Generally you have to purchase the rider at the same time you purchase your annuity contract, and if you violate any of the rider requirements, the whole guaranteed income deal for which you've been paying extra money is off.

Generally, an annuity is a better idea for people who have already maxed out their other retirement plan options. If you do buy one, don't sink all of your money into an annuity. It's nice to have another guaranteed source of income during retirement right along with Social Security and, if you're lucky, pension benefits.

But as a general rule, you want to keep your money diversified among several investment options. That's why the investment industry is so fond of the phrase, "Don't put all of your eggs in one basket."

HEAD OF HOUSEHOLD TIPS: RETIREMENT INCOME PLANNING

- Determine your personal goals. Consider when and where you want to retire, what type of lifestyle you want to lead, and try to figure out how much that will cost.

- As a rule of thumb, estimate that you'll need approximately 70–80 percent of your preretirement annual income for each year during retirement. If you're a woman, in particular, don't forget to factor in the costs of medical insurance and long-term care, because women tend to live longer than men.

- Many retirees today are reporting that they're spending even more money in retirement than they did when they were working. Yikes.

- Make it a goal to pay off your house before you retire. This will reduce your cost of living requirement substantially.

- Determine your retirement benefit levels—check your employer's retirement plan and contact Social Security to determine your income payments. You should receive a PEBS—Personal Earnings and Benefits Estimate Statement—every year around your birthday with an estimate of your retirement benefits. You can also request this online at http://ssa.gov.

- Maximize your savings by utilizing tax-deferred investments, such as IRAs, employer retirement plans, and annuities.

- Continue to stay invested throughout retirement. You don't want to just spend down all of your money, because you might run out. If you stay invested, your money has the opportunity to continue growing to help keep up with the rising cost of living.

Financial Advisors

Few people try to buy a home without the aid of a real estate agent. Fewer still try to self-diagnose an ear infection without a doctor or sue their neighbors without a lawyer. So why try to manage something as important as your finances without the expert advice of a professional?

There are so many different types of investments available today, and the Internet is literally flooded with information that can boggle and confuse the best of us. That's why, for single parents in particular who have way too many competing priorities, it can help to consult with a professional who knows the industry and has experience pairing investments with investors. A well-trained financial advisor can

- Help you assess your current financial health by examining your assets, liabilities, income, insurance, taxes, investments, and estate plan;
- Help you set realistic financial goals;
- Provide you with a written financial plan, put it into action, and monitor its progress;
- Help you stay on track to meet your financial goals in light of changing personal circumstances, investment vehicles, market environments, and tax laws.

Where to Look

Just as you would search for a doctor or dentist, the best place to seek out referrals is from your family, friends, and business associates.

Other good sources of referrals include attorneys, insurance agents, accountants, and bankers, who are generally tied to your local financial community and have a large referral network. You may also contact the following agencies to help you find a qualified financial planner in your area:

- Financial Planning Association
- National Association of Personal Financial Advisors
- American Society of CLU and ChFC
- Certified Financial Planner Board of Standards

You may check out the disciplinary history of a financial advisor to find out if disgruntled clients or regulatory agencies have filed any complaints against him or her by contacting FINRA BrokerCheck (www.finra.org/brokercheck).

What to Ask

Once you've obtained a shortlist of a few potential advisors, schedule face-to face interviews in order to ask questions and establish your comfort level with this person. This first consult should be free of charge.

It's important to have a rapport with your financial advisor, just like you would with a doctor or a dentist. First off the bat, be wary of people who overpromise things like outrageous investment returns.

Below is a list of questions appropriate for you to ask a financial planner. Recognize that you are entitled to ask as many questions as necessary to make you feel comfortable, and the advisor has an obligation to answer those questions if he or she wants your business.

- What educational degrees, financial licenses, and designations do you hold?
- What is your work background and experience?
- How long have you been a personal financial advisor?
- Are you licensed to sell all types of financial products, including life insurance and securities?
- What is your basic approach to financial planning? Do you provide a written plan?
- Do you have an area of specialization?
- Do you handle personal tax returns?
- What types of clients do you serve, and do you have a minimum net worth or income requirement?
- Will you be the only person working with me?
- How do you get paid for your services (sales commission, hourly fee?) and how much do you typically charge?
- Do you have any business relationships or partnerships that may pose a conflict of interest?
- Have you ever been disciplined for unlawful or unethical actions in your professional career?

What to Expect

Once you've selected an advisor, expect the tables to be turned. This time, you'll be expected to answer a lot of questions—about your age, marital status, current financial picture, level of debt, children and/or step-children and their plans (to see if you need to save for college), parents (to see if you may be responsible for their elder care), current income and prospects for the future, and even alimony and palimony payments.

HEAD OF HOUSEHOLD TIP: TEST AN ADVISOR

Note that an advisor may not have all the answers you're seeking. The occasional "I don't know, but I'll find out" can be a reassuring indicator that this person will work on your behalf to address all of your concerns. Consider purposely asking a question that bears a little research, just to find out if and how quickly he or she responds after your initial meeting.

These questions may seem intrusive at first, but that's why it's so important to make sure you select an advisor with whom you're comfortable sharing this information.

A good financial advisor should hold your hand throughout the initial profiling process. Choose someone who will help you become familiar with investment news, talk to you regularly about money and opportunities, and help you save and invest automatically every month.

Unless you grant discretionary authority, your advisor must have your permission to buy and sell stocks, bonds, and any other investments on your behalf. As a general rule, it's not a good idea to grant discretionary authority, even under limited guidelines.

If you suspect a financial advisor has abused your trust, you have certain rights and recourse. There are generally two levels of regulatory action: Your state's consumer fraud division within your local district attorney's office, and at the federal level FINRA, the largest independent regulator for all securities firms doing business in the United States.

HEAD OF HOUSEHOLD TIP: FINANCIAL ADVISOR CREDENTIALS

The title your money mentor goes by can tell you a lot about his experience and qualifications. There are financial consultants, advisors, planners, accountants, and a plethora of acronyms to describe these professionals.

While CFPs and CFAs require at least three years of professional experience and must have successfully passed one or more exams, "financial planners" can range from the highly qualified to your Uncle Eddy, the used car dealer. In fact, many banks, mutual fund, and insurance companies call their advisors "financial consultants," but they're really just sales people.

Make sure you choose a licensed, qualified financial planner who is subject to state and federal regulatory agencies. The following financial designation glossary may help you decipher various educational degrees and licenses these professionals hold:

- Chartered Financial Analyst (CFA)—An investment professional who has passed examinations in economics, financial accounting, portfolio management, security analysis, and standards of conduct, with a minimum of three years' work experience in the investment industry.

- Certified Financial Planner (CFP)—A financial planner who has completed study and passed examinations in risk management, investments, tax planning, retirement planning, and estate planning. Must have a minimum level of three years' experience, continue to update knowledge in the field, and adhere to prescribed code of ethics.

- Chartered Financial Consultant (ChFC)—An insurance professional with a focus on financial planning who has completed courses in economics, investments, insurance, taxation, and related areas, and must complete 30 continuing education credits every two years.

- Chartered Life Underwriter (CLU)—A life insurance agent who has passed a national examination in insurance and related subjects, and must complete 30 continuing education credits every two years.

- Certified Public Accountant (CPA)—An experienced accountant who has met education, statutory, and licensing requirements of the state in which he or she resides, including 120 hours of continuing professional education.

- Personal Financial Specialist (PFS)—A CPA who has passed a financial planning exam and offers a broad range of personal financial services, which may include investment advice, and may obtain the CPA/PFS designation.

- Juris Doctor (law degree; JD)—A graduate from a law school. JDs may become an attorney licensed to practice law within a state or multiple states after passing a cumulative state bar exam.

- Master of Business Administration (MBA)—A graduate degree, preferably with concentrations in financial planning and estate planning.

- Doctorate (PhD)—An academic degree that indicates a high, if not the highest, level of academic achievement conferred by a university. Requires at least three years of graduate study beyond the bachelor's and/or master's degree and demonstrated original research via a formal dissertation.

TEN

Saving

Yet again, saving money is about values. With some noteworthy exceptions, people don't normally buy things they don't want or need. They buy things they value. They pay the price they feel is a good exchange for that value—sometimes maybe a little more; when we're lucky—a little less.

So in order to save money more effectively, it's imperative to examine your values. Here are some ideas to help you investigate this topic more closely—for you and your family.

1. Make a list of the things that are important to you (not just monetary things).
2. Make a list of the things you tend to like to do or buy that cost money. Be specific; look in your home, closet, garage, or jewelry box to help you.
3. Make a list of all the things that you've been wanting to buy, and/or hope to buy in the next six months.
4. Make a separate list of long-term wishes; things you hope to buy in the next year to five years.
5. Make a list of all the things you would like to buy within the next 25 years.
6. Look at your lists and pick out the things that will be important for you to still own on your dying bed.
7. Compare your first list—the list of all the things that are important to you—with all of your other lists. Which list has more things that will still be important to you on your deathbed?

8. Now here's the real values revealer: Ask your children to repeat all the steps you just took above.

The values you embrace will be the ones you teach your children. You may not need to make those lists to recognize where your values currently lie, and you probably have a good idea of areas where you can cut back to jump-start a more aggressive savings plan.

SAVING FOR MATERNITY LEAVE

What you save your money for is a matter of priority. Personally, I always wanted children. I always wanted a career. I always wanted to be able to stay home as long as possible when my children were first born. Unfortunately, that concept of finding the right guy and getting married was a little further down the priority list. Which left me with a tall challenge: Having babies on my own, raising babies on my own, staying home with my babies as long as possible. The nice thing, however, about having a tall order in life is that your priorities become very clear.

My first "real" job out of college was perfect—an advertising copywriter at a radio station. I was paid a "real" salary that amounted to $5 an hour. Whoohoo. So I waited tables on the weekends, earning more in two shifts than I did in a 40-hour work week. I saved my paychecks and lived on my tips. Two years later, after I had my first child, I was able to live off my savings for six months before I went out and found another (higher-paying) job. If I could do that making five bucks an hour, I always wondered about women executives who take six weeks maternity leave and are back at work before baby is even sleeping through the night. Frankly, that just sounds exhausting to me.

Fast forward 14 years. I had been freelancing for 4 years, and just wrapped up my biggest income-earning year and had a pretty big war chest saved. I considered it a sign from the gods, so I decided to have another baby. I managed to stay home with him for one full year before having to return to face the war-ravaged halls of corporate America again.

Yes, I could be driving a nicer car with automatic windows (although my biceps would be smaller). I could live in a bigger house (although it would take more time and money to keep it clean and maintained). I could have a bigger investment portfolio (although I would have lost most of it in the fall of 2008; but it would've come back). Instead, on my dying deathbed, I'm going to cherish the memory of my son waking from his morning nap, silently climbing out of his crib (before he could walk), crawling into the kitchen where I stood with the door open staring absently into the fridge (as new moms are prone to do), then looking over at that beautiful five-month old face that wistfully said, "Bah." Bottle. Yay.

Saving money helps define your values. What you spend it on helps define your priorities.

A WORD ABOUT WOMEN AND SAVING

The number one reason women need more retirement savings than men is very simply because we tend to live longer. On average, a man who reaches age 65 is likely to live to at least age 80, while a woman is more likely to live to age 84 or longer. In fact, 30 percent of all women aged 65 can expect to reach 90 years old or older.

Women need to be more aggressive savers because they are less likely to receive as large a pension, if any at all. According to the Department of Labor, the median pension for women is about half that of men. Yeah, that's right, half. Not to mention that more women than men work for employers that do not provide retirement benefits through either a pension or 401(k) savings plan.

How can this be, when women have made such strides in joining the workforce and earning higher and higher salaries? The problem, it appears, is the trade-off. While women have certainly engaged in shouldering more income responsibility, most have not shirked their traditional duties.

In other words, women are still birthing the babies, largely responsible for their upbringing, and typically serve as primary caregiver for today's onslaught of aging parents. Single or not (and it's so much harder to juggle these burdens when you're a single parent), women have taken on more without a proportionate trade-off in home-front responsibilities.

And when you're a single parent, there is no one to trade off with anyway. All the responsibility is yours.

Although pension and Social Security laws don't care if you're a man or a woman, payments are based on your level of pay and the number of years you worked. Needless to say, benefits favor men when you consider that 50 percent of women quit working for some time in their careers to care for children, parents, or other family members, compared to only 1 percent of men. To make matters worse, consider these figures:

• Women spend an average of 32 years in the workforce compared with 44 years for men, and are more than twice as likely to work on a part-time basis.

- Women who work full time earn about 77¢ for every dollar men earn, but that's mainly just during the early years.
- During the ages of 45–54, women earn only 74 percent of men's earnings and 73 percent during the ages of 55–64.
- Since women can't save money they haven't earned, their median Social Security benefit is 70 percent that of men and pension income almost half.
- Social Security benefits represent virtually all of the income that 4 out of 10 single women over age 65 in the United States receive.
- More than two-thirds of unmarried elderly women would be living below the poverty line if they did not receive Social Security.
- Divorce reduces wealth on average by 77 percent.
- Divorced women often experience the greatest drop in their standard of living once they retire.

The result? Women 65 and older are twice as likely as their male counterparts to have incomes at or below the national poverty level, currently $7,800 a year for single people. In fact, 75 percent of all elderly poor are women, according to the U.S. Census Bureau.

HEAD OF HOUSEHOLD TIP: LIVE TOGETHER?

If you live with your partner but never marry, you need to be aware of what benefits you qualify for in retirement.

If one partner stays home and does not establish a substantial long-term employment record, his or her situation is particularly precarious. Should the couple remain together, the stay-home partner would not be eligible for any Social Security benefits at retirement age. Should the couple split up, not only would he or she not be eligible for Social Security, but entitled to only half the household assets—assuming that his or her name is on the mortgage and other major assets.

Your choices are simple. Earn 40 quarters/credits of work history (about 10 years) in order to qualify for your own Social Security benefits. Or, get married and stay married for at least 10 years to qualify for your partner's benefits. Otherwise, you'd better be independently wealthy and not require any government benefits during retirement.

PARENT AND SINGLE PARENT DISCRIMINATION IN THE WORKPLACE

According to the Center for WorkLife Law, mothers are 79 percent less likely to be hired, 100 percent less likely to be promoted, and are offered starting salaries that average $11,000 less than those of women without children.

If the employment environment is tough on mothers in general—representing 82 percent of American women—imagine how much tougher it is for a single mom. Actually, you probably don't have to imagine this at all.

Job discrimination is not limited to moms, either. According to the Center, fathers who take a more active role in caregiving are also penalized on the job in the form of blocked promotions or lower performance ratings.

With 79 million baby boomers retiring over the next 20 years, there's more than parent discrimination at stake. Moms and Dads will bear the responsibility of caring for or seeing to the care of their elderly parents. For a single parent, the burden is that much more difficult—being responsible for both children and elderly parents without a partner or second income for support. This generation of caregivers has been dubbed "the sandwich generation" because they are sandwiched in the middle of two needy demographics.

For single parents, it's more like the "smashed generation." The burden of caregiving for these two diverse groups of dependents is likely to be overwhelming—emotionally, physically, and financially.

WHAT YOU CAN DO

As it turns out, single parenting forces you to develop skills well beyond or at least at a higher level of competency than your average single or married peers.

First of all, the longer you've been a single parent, the more you've learned to rely on yourself to provide for your family and not expect any person or government entity to rush to your aid.

Second, if such resources do exist to support you, financially or otherwise, chances are you have found them and learned to tap them adequately and judiciously.

Third, your forced values system has taught you to triage priorities—knowing instinctively when faced with dilemmas which challenges are more important to accomplish, and which can be left undone. Simply letting go of some of your responsibilities, and understanding the ramifications of doing so, is one of the most important skills a single parent can develop.

When you juggle priorities, you have to be able to discern which are more important than others. Some "priorities" are simply never achieved. For example, work demands are more important than house-cleaning demands. Some things, like dinner on the table every night, persist continuously; so if dinner becomes cereal with milk once in awhile, no harm done.

Typical Conversation in My Household

Child: What's for dinner?

Me: Again? I made dinner for you last night. What . . . you want it every night?

As your elder care responsibilities begin to step up, you will face the constant challenge of weighing your child's needs versus your parents', and somewhere in there you'll need to find time to take care of your own needs. Just remember that people are more important than money, places, things, and activities. So if you need to cut back on ballet lessons for your daughter so the two of you can spend Saturdays caring for your parents, remember that this was the natural order of things way back in "the olden days."

No harm will come to your children by spending time with and caring for grandparents, yucky as that prospect may seem to your children. Give your children one or more specific "jobs" related to caregiving, so that they are truly involved in the process and learn to take pride in owning a responsibility. Set expectations for behavior and attitude. Reward them with free time and your expressed gratitude (not money), and make sure they understand how important they are to holding together and nurturing the family unit.

What they miss in soccer, ballet, baseball, or piano training, your children will learn in the value of human life. As these decisions come into play, reassess how you and your children spend your time and money. You may find that cutting back on birthday parties in lieu of spending time with an invalid grandparent can be enjoyable. It's about changing your mind-set to prioritize and enjoy the things that truly matter.

Once you employ this mind-set, you will pass this on to your children by example. This value set can also help you financially by prioritizing what is important and saving money on what is not. Not to mention the fact that, as a single parent, it is even more critical that your children recognize and take responsibility for caring for a senior parent (that would be *you*, in the future).

EXPERIENCED AND WELL-QUALIFIED

By the same token, single parents are well equipped with the qualities it takes to manage business and financial matters. Recognize that you do this all day, every day, all by yourself.

By the same token, your solo burden is also your exclusive opportunity to make decisions based on your values, without having to consider anyone other than yourself and your children. This can be quite liberating, but it takes a certain discipline to be good at it. It's important to understand that you don't have to keep up with other people, you don't need to acquire the same things or take the same vacations or do things in quite the same way.

As the sole adult in your family, you don't *have* to make decisions by yourself.

You get to.

TACTICS FOR SAVING MONEY

Take Advantage of Lower Interest Rates

The economy moves in cycles, so periodically—depending on market conditions—the Federal Reserve will chip away at interest rates until the economy starts to take notice. The Fed meets every six weeks, sometimes more, to determine whether or not to raise or lower the discount and federal funds rate. By increasing or decreasing these rates, over time the Fed can impact practically every other interest rate charged by U.S. banks, including the interest rates on car loans, mortgages, credit cards, CD and savings accounts, and business loans.

By controlling interest rates, the Fed controls the amount of money we as consumers have available to spend. When it lowers rates, money may be borrowed more cheaply, consumers spend the money, and the economy is energized. Conversely, when the Fed raises rates, it puts the brakes on consumer spending and the economy slows down as a means to avoid inflation.

During low-interest rate periods, consider your opportunities to take advantage of the pro-spending climate.

Buy High-Ticket Items at the Right Time

If you've been contemplating buying a new car (or at least new to you), a low-interest rate environment may be the time to take the plunge.

Car dealers and other manufacturers of expensive toys (boats, jet skis, etc.) tend to offer low financing rates during these periods to attract traditionally more conservative consumers. Even if money is tight, this may still be the right time to make a great finance deal—particularly if you're willing to walk away from the transaction if it does not suit you perfectly.

Remember that the worst time to buy a car is when yours just died and you absolutely have to buy a new one. This situation reduces your negotiating leverage. Just as the best time to look for a new job is while you already have one, low interest rates create a favorable climate to start considering purchases that you will eventually have to make anyway.

Try to anticipate your needs when interest rates are low. The last thing you want to do is buy a car when you're too stressed out to negotiate a good price and interest rates are on an upswing, to boot.

Timing a Home Improvement Loan

By the same token, if you've been thinking of adding on to or renovating your home, consider the best time to get a great interest rate on a home improvement loan. A home improvement loan uses the equity in your home to generate cash for housing improvements and renovations, and the interest is also tax deductible.

Consider home improvements that will add equity to your home's resale value, such as installing central air-conditioning or adding a multipurpose den/bedroom with closet.

SAVE MONEY ON YOUR MORTGAGE BY PAYING IT OFF FASTER

At the front end of a mortgage, 95 percent of your payments go to interest. The faster you can pay off your mortgage, the more money you will save.

There are several strategies that can help you save money on your home mortgage over the long term. I'm not talking about the nickel-and-dime stuff; you can save serious amounts of money.

Strategy #1: Increase Your Monthly Payment

By adding an additional $100 to your mortgage payment with instructions to direct it toward paying down your principal, you can save a lot more money than you might expect. See for yourself.

- $250,000 mortgage loan
- 7 percent interest rate
- 30-year term

By paying only the required $1,663 a month, you will end up paying $348,772 in interest alone over the 30-year period. However, if you pay out an additional $100 each month ($1,763), you would pay off the loan nearly five years earlier and save $66,780 in interest.

You read that correctly: $66,780 saved.

Strategy #2: Biweekly Payment Program

There's an easier way to reduce the interest you pay and doesn't involve coughing up additional money each month: Automatic biweekly payments. This is actually quite helpful from a day-to-day budgeting standpoint as well, as you pay half your mortgage every two weeks instead of once a month. This way a smaller chunk of a biweekly paycheck goes to your mortgage, leaving you a more even balance throughout the month to pay other bills and expenses.

When you pay every two weeks instead of once a month, you chip away at your mortgage balance a little faster. Since interest is applied to the amount still owed, you owe slightly less every two weeks, so you save more interest than you do paying once a month. See for yourself.

- $250,000 mortgage loan
- 7 percent interest rate
- 30-year term

Again, by paying only the required $1,663 a month, you will end up paying $348,772 in interest alone over the 30-year period.

By making split payments of $831.63 every two weeks, you will save $88,875 in interest and pay off your mortgage seven years earlier. Yay.

Strategy #3: Increase Monthly Payment + Biweekly Payment Program

Let's say you get crazy and combine these two strategies. Compare your savings:

- $250,000 mortgage loan
- 7 percent interest rate
- 30-year term

By paying only the required $1,663 a month, you will end up paying $348,772 in interest alone over the 30-year period.

If you make biweekly payments with an additional $100 toward principal each month, you would save $120,240 in interest and pay off the loan nine years earlier. Wow. Double yay.

Here are these numbers in a comparison grid. Make a copy and stick this on your refrigerator to remind you to stay focused on long-term savings goals and forgo impulse trips to the mall. You can use any number of online mortgage calculators to customize these numbers to reflect your own situation and make your own table.

Table E   Mortgage Payoff Grid: $250,000 Mortgage @ 7% Interest on 30-Year Term

Payment strategy	Interest saved ($)	Years till paid off
Regular mortgage payment once a month	0.00	30 years
Pay additional $100 a month toward principal	66,780.00	24 years, 10 months
Regular mortgage payment in biweekly payments	88,875.00	23 years
Biweekly payments + $100 a month	120,240.00	21 years

The biweekly payment strategy is offered by many mortgage lenders and usually incurs a fee to set up ($150–400), plus a nominal ($5 or more) fee per payment received. These fees, within reason, are worth it in saved interest over the long term. Note that a biweekly payment program will likely require an automatic transfer from you bank account, rather you manually making the payments.

Also be aware that some lenders may impose prepayment penalties if you try to pay your mortgage off early.

One caution about the biweekly payment strategy: No more "free" paychecks. Because employers typically pay biweekly and there are 52 weeks in the year, twice a year you usually get a "free" paycheck—totaling three for the month. Since the biweekly mortgage payment system is set up on this same schedule, your mortgage payments will automatically transfer every two weeks, soaking up much of the "free" money you might have previously used at your own discretion.

You should try to engage in a biweekly payment program as early as possible upon buying a home, before you pay in a load of interest in those first few years on each payment. However, you can typically start at any time and will still see significant long-term savings.

Other than the up-front fee, a biweekly payment program is pretty painless and doesn't require that you commit more money to your mortgage than you would without it. However, the savings are quite significant.

Strategy #4: One Additional Mortgage Payment a Year

You can get the same results of the biweekly payment strategy by instead making one extra mortgage payment a year. If you believe you are disciplined enough to make an extra payment in one lump sum (and a good use for your "free" paychecks), write a separate check for it and indicate that it should be applied toward your mortgage principal.

Homeowners should also weigh the wisdom of paying off a mortgage early against investing the extra money. The early payoff seems to have a particular appeal to women, who tend to be more conservative investors and feel more security and peace of mind from owning a home outright.

Strategy #5: Finance or Refinance with a 15-Year Mortgage

If you have the resources to make extra payments to your mortgage principal, consider instead financing or refinancing your home with a 15-year mortgage loan. Unfortunately, your interest rate will be only slightly lower, and your payments much higher. However, you'll own your home outright in just 15 years and save a ton in interest. Under the same scenario, here's how you would stack up:

- $250,000 mortgage loan
- 6.75 percent interest rate
- 15-year term

With a mortgage payment of $2,212 a month, you would end up paying $148,209 in interest over the 15-year period as compared to the $348,772 in interest for monthly payments on a 30-year term. That's a savings of more than $200,000 over a 30-year term mortgage.

While you're at it, you might as well pay your 15-year mortgage with the biweekly payment program. In this case, you would pay only $129,010 in interest by splitting your mortgage into biweekly payments.

It's hard to imagine that you could be paying about $350,000 in interest over the life of your mortgage. To you, it's just a big chunk out of your monthly income. But when you add up the numbers, you'll discover that it's a much larger chunk out of your potential lifetime savings.

That's the magic of compounding interest over time. With debt it works against you; but with investing, it can work in your favor.

GENDER-BLIND CAR SHOPPING

A Yale University study found that women pay anywhere from $200 to $400 more for new cars than men. For generations, single women have had to endure trying rounds of negotiations and pressure from car salespeople—usually men—who see them as an easy mark.

Well, the Internet has changed all that. The nice thing about shopping for a car online is that it's gender-neutral and you can get exactly what you want without being subjected to sales pressure. To help you find the vehicle to match your needs, supplement any field research at local dealers by logging on to popular sites such as *Consumer Reports* and www.Edmunds.com.

You can also visit such popular car buying sites as www.carmax.com, www.autobytel.com, or www.autotrader.com to start searching for your car. You can do everything but take a test drive without any chatter or pressure from a salesman.

Single Mom Auto Repair Confession

As a young single mom, I occasionally asked a male friend to accompany me to an auto repair shop. This is because, despite the fact that we were discussing my car, the mechanic would always talk to the man rather than to me. As aggravating as it was to endure this, it helped me accomplish my primary goal—saving money. I would always end up paying just for the one repair using this strategy than when I went in by myself—when inevitably there was always an additional problem that needed repair, cleaning, or replacement.

SAVE FOR VACATION: FAMILY STYLE

This can be a fun way to teach your children the value of saving and careful spending. Make it a family project to save energy in your household. Then use the myriad of tips below to work together to realize savings—specifically in the energy category.

First, go online, visit AAA, or the library to help you pick a family vacation spot. Keep searching until you find the one thing that everyone can get excited about. Estimate your costs. Every bit of money you save will be applied to your family vacation fund—preferably via a separate bank account in which your children can help you make deposits and watch that account grow. Some banks and credit unions offer "Club Accounts" to allow you to save for a specific purpose.

Once you hit your vacation goal, take the vacation (or as soon as practical). Call it your energy savings vacation. You can use this strategy for a lot of household purchases, including a WII if that's what your children really want.

Voila: Values.

Determine How Much Energy You Use

Just as you wouldn't try to establish a household budget without examining your current spending habits, the first step to saving energy is to determine how much you presently use.

For general reference, the Department of Energy estimates the national average household energy use at:

Figure A   Household Energy

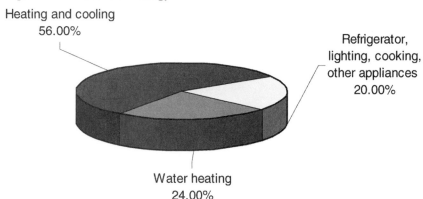

Heating and cooling
56.00%

Refrigerator, lighting, cooking, other appliances
20.00%

Water heating
24.00%

Visit the Lawrence Berkeley Lab at http://homeenergysaver.lbl.gov to launch a computer program that can estimate your annual energy use. By answering a smattering of questions about your home's energy use, you can receive an estimated calculation of your heating, cooling, hot water, lights, and appliance use.

You can also measure your energy use by gathering up all your utility bills, check registers, or online records over the past year and adding them up to determine areas where you can cut back the most. Mild or harsh winter and summer seasons can make a big difference in your usage each year, as can cyclical soaring gas and electric prices.

But again, knowledge is power. By identifying where most of your money goes, you and your family can focus on areas where the biggest cutbacks can have the maximum impact on your household expenses.

Lower Your Heating/Cooling Bills

The following are several tips specifically designed to help save heating and cooling costs within your home without paying out extra money:

- Make sure the fireplace flue is closed during summer months so your AC doesn't get sucked up the chimney.
- Lower the thermostat at night during winter months.
- Wrap an insulating cover around your water heater.
- Ensure that all heating and cooling vents are clear.
- Line dry your laundry in lieu of using the dryer.
- Inquire as to whether your utility companies offer lower rates for off-peak hours—which may mean doing laundry at midnight.
- When you turn on your air conditioner for the first time, or after a vacation, or during a hot spell, don't set the thermostat any colder than normal, as it will not cool your home any faster.
- Don't place lamps or TV sets near your air-conditioning thermostat. The thermostat senses heat from these appliances, which can cause the air conditioner to run longer than necessary.
- Plant trees or shrubs to shade air-conditioning units but not to block the airflow. A unit operating in the shade uses as much as 10 percent less electricity than the same one operating in the sun.
- Replace standard lightbulbs with electric-efficient fluorescent bulbs (as these bulbs are more expensive, don't replace the ones in light fixtures that have a tendency to get knocked over).
- Cook with small appliances instead of your oven or stove top. Microwave ovens are the most energy efficient, but other less expensive alternatives include toaster ovens, slow cookers, and pressure cookers.

- Consider three-way lamps and bulbs; they make it easier to keep lighting levels low when brighter light is not necessary.
- Position your refrigerator away from direct sunlight and close contact with hot appliances that will make the compressor work harder.

Many utility companies offer "level pay" billing plans that average your annual usage and bill you fixed payments each month. This allows you to spread out your peak season costs (i.e., high air-conditioning bills in summer, high heating bills in winter). This can be helpful if you're trying to maintain a monthly budget all year long.

However, be aware that at year-end the utility company will "balance bill" you for any excess amount used. It can be difficult to pay off an unexpected large bill like this, so anticipate wisely and practice conserving energy all year round.

TEACH YOUR CHILDREN TO EARN AND MANAGE MONEY

Today, children tend to learn the value of money at an earlier age. They grow up faster, the toys are more sophisticated, and let's face it: There's just a lot more to want. To want to buy. Like keeping pace with video game technology. What's an overextended single parent to do?

Put the children to work. It's not unprecedented you know. In the olden days (as my son calls them), parents used to have large families just to get all the work done around the farm. Children used to milk cows and feed chickens and spit-shine their boots before they walked three miles to school. So I really don't think it's too much to ask your child to take his or her plate off the table and load the dishes.

One strategy is to establish "member-of-family" chores. These are chores expected to be completed in exchange for the mere honor of being a member of the family. In other words, you don't get paid diddly-squat for doing them.

Then there's the regular household work. This is where you pay your children in order to teach them about the value of money. And don't think your nine-year-old is too young to clean the toilet; he's not and it's kind of fun, actually. These are very learnable tasks. You figure if your child can take out 26 aliens in his quest for video game glory, he can certainly run a dust cloth across the furniture.

In addition to earning discretionary income, your children learn good values and logistical life skills. For example, imagine a son who can go off to college and already know how to wash his laundry. Do not underestimate the power of the buck. You can pay your children less money than you'd have to pay a maid, and yet look at all the pertinent benefits. If you work out of an office at home, these janitorial expenses may even be tax deductible.

There's a part two to this scenario. There is absolutely no point in paying your children for work completed if you're then going to go out and buy all of their toys. This will not instill the value of money. They have to learn to spend their earnings wisely. When junior learns he has to buy his own basketball, he is a little less hasty to grab the most expensive one. And gone are the can-I-haves in the grocery store checkout line. Teach the credo:

"You want it, you buy it."

Encourage saving for long-term goals. If your son wants a wet suit or some other big-ticket item, agree to pay for half. First go shopping to see how much the item costs and to get your child properly motivated. Then go home and devise a work and fee schedule—as well as timeline. The time-line is important, because the younger the child the less time it should take to achieve her goal, or she'll become frustrated and quit. The added advantage of a child buying her own toys is that she is more likely to take good care of them, knowing that she will have to come up with the bucks to replace them.

Scheming for Mario Kart

My youngest son recently lost one of his handheld video game car-tridges. I fussed and worried over this for weeks, but he seemed uncon-cerned and that was unusual for him. Then one Friday after I gave him his allowance, he smiled big and tore up to his room, calling out "I almost have enough money saved to buy Mario Kart!" I had no idea he was saving to replace the game he had lost. He'd never asked me to buy it, and I certainly never offered. But yay, right?

If you don't think your children would ever go for this, cut them off— cold turkey. Let them know that any big-ticket items they want in between birthdays and Christmas, they will have to buy for themselves. Post a chore list and accompanying pay on the fridge. It's funny that the more arduous the task (and higher the pay), the more often it is completed.

If you get them started early enough, children actually like doing grown-up chores. And by the time they reach adolescence, they accept that chores are a part of life and might actually be pretty good at them. After all, practice makes perfect.

Big Bucks for a Big Job

As a youngster, my son liked to clean out the inside of the refrigerator. It was a big-ticket item and he initiated it on his own, at least twice a year.

HEAD OF HOUSEHOLD TIP: SAVING DAILY

- Take $5 from your wallet every day and put it in a safe place. That will add up to $1,825 in a year. Vacation in a coffee can. Yay.
- Write down a financial goal on a piece of paper. Cut that piece of paper into a size of a dollar bill, with the goal clearly written in large letters. Place that paper in your wallet with your money, and read it every time you reach for your bills. Once you've reached that goal, replace it with another.

ELEVEN

Succession

Writing a will is one of those tasks most people keep meaning to do but procrastinate. And no wonder. It's like buying life insurance or a funeral plot; no one wants to face their own mortality. No one wants to plan on not being alive.

Multiply this very normal fear by about thousandfold, and that's how a single parent with no "ex" (or no "ex" they can trust) feels. The dreaded "O" word—"orphan"—comes to mind. Hopefully, you have family that will care for your children should something happen to you. But still, when children born of married couples lose a parent, they've got another to spare. Not so with a single parent.

That, of course, is why it's all the more critical that you proactively plan for your own demise. Can you even imagine your 14-year-old trying to make decisions about an open or closed casket? The stuff of nightmares.

Of all the financial planning a single parent must take on—saving, investing, budgeting—succession planning is by far the scariest and the one you are most likely to procrastinate.

For the sake of your family, write your will today detailing what should happen in the wake of your death.

YOUR WILL

A will is the legal document where you name both the guardian for your children and the executor of your estate. It is necessary to control who will inherit your property, your assets, and even your children upon your death. When it comes to wills, keep in mind that

- The will must be typewritten or computer generated (unless it is a holographic will, and we'll get to that);
- The document must expressly state that it's your will;
- You must date and sign the will;
- The will must be signed by at least two (in some states, three) witnesses who won't inherit anything under the will. Although they don't need to read it, they should watch you sign the will.

You don't have to have your will notarized, although in many states it can help simplify the court procedures required to prove the validity of the will after you die. Nor does a will need to be recorded or filed with any government agency; simply keep your will in a safe, accessible place and be sure your will's executor knows where it is.

If you have a high net worth or any potential complications, then it may be best to have a competent attorney help you draft a will or at least review it for you. However, you don't necessarily need an attorney to draft a will. You can draft your own will with the aid of a last will and testament kit or software program.

Handwritten wills, called "holographic" wills, are legal in about half the states in the United States. To be valid, a holographic will must be written, dated, and signed in the handwriting of the person making the will. You do not necessarily have to have the will witnessed for it to be recognized as legal. You can check out whether your state recognizes a holographic will at http://www.lawchek.com/Library1/_books/probate/qanda/holographic.htm.

HEAD OF HOUSEHOLD TIP: ACT RIGHT NOW

If you don't have a will, write a holographic will right now. No really, put down this book and write it right now and come back to the book. It doesn't have to be long, just hit the highlights. When you finally get around to writing a more formal will, you can destroy this handwritten one. (You can always draft the holographic will on your computer and then copy it by hand.) If you go ahead and get this one out the way—which honestly could take less than 10 minutes—then the toughest part is over. You've faced it and you've dealt with it and you know the things you need to think about further. And you've at least taken the first step to securing your children's future. That's worth 10 minutes.

PROBATE

If you don't create a will to transfer your property when you die, state law will determine what happens to your property. This is called "intestate." When there's no will, there's the chance that a part of your estate may go to the state instead of your family.

TYPES OF WILLS

If you're of sound mind and legal age, you should have a will. Married couples typically name each other as beneficiaries using a Reciprocal Will. The Nuncupative Will is oral. While you often see them in the movies, video- or audio-taped wills are not currently recognized by any U.S. state—legally speaking they're simply window dressing to accompany the written will.

You may have also heard of the Living Will, but that's not quite the same thing. A Living Will is a written instruction to terminate medical attempts to prolong your life in a terminally ill situation; it has no impact after your death.

EXECUTOR

You should name an executor of your will and estate, also called a "personal representative." Normally this is a relative or close friend whom you choose to probate your estate and carry out the provisions of your will. With a simple estate this is generally not a difficult role, as the executor typically retains an attorney to process the necessary probate forms. The main role of the executor is to be trustworthy and committed to carrying out your wishes.

Some states require that the executor be a resident of that state, while others will allow a relative from another state to assume the role. Your executor must be of legal age, so you may not name underage children to this position. Also, be sure your candidate is willing to take on the responsibility and be sure to name an alternate executor in case he or she is unable to serve.

GUARDIAN

If, as the head of your household, there is no other parent to care for your children in the event of your untimely death, you will need to choose a guardian. A guardian basically takes the place of you as a parent, so be sure to select someone who can offer the best care for your children. This is often a close relative. Also, have a conversation with your candidate to ensure he or she is willing to accept the responsibility.

It is also a good idea to name an alternate guardian should the primary guardian be unable to take on the responsibility. This isn't as unlikely as you may think: Consider the scenario where your sister, your named guardian, and you are both killed in a car accident during an outing together.

If you don't want your ex (be it spouse or otherwise biological parent of the child) to get custody upon your death, you'll need to take preemptive steps now. Even a noncustodial surviving parent can get custody unless the court finds the person has abandoned the children or is unfit as a parent.

You may think your child's biological parent is out of the picture for life—perhaps he or she has a history of violence, substance abuse, criminal record, or may just be chronically irresponsible and a poor choice for parent. Maybe he doesn't even know the child exists or that it is his biological offspring.

These factors do not necessarily eliminate this person from gaining custody of your child upon your death—when you can no longer do anything about it. The fact is courts give preference to biological parents unless they have reason not to.

Consider, too, that if you have children with different biological parents, your children may be split up upon your death to go live with their respective parents. You may not feel that's in their best interest.

If something needs to be done to ensure the other biological parent does not get custody of your child upon your death, now is the time to do it. Morose or not, death can come at any time. Ensure your child's future is protected.

You should most certainly use your will to name your choice of guardian and include an explanation of why he or she is a better choice than the surviving biological parent. If you can document willful abandonment and refusal to pay child support, include that as well. By all means, seek professional advice from an attorney who specializes in this area.

If, on the other hand, you do want your former spouse or biological parent to get custody, be sure to say so in your will. Otherwise one of your family members may initiate litigation to gain custody of your children. This could set off a nasty battle that would benefit no one, certainly not your children, who need as much family as possible going forward—and need them to get along.

BEQUESTS

Lastly, you'll want to name your beneficiaries within the bequests section of the will. Remember that you should name contingent entities for each of these roles (executor, guardian, and even beneficiaries) should one of them die before you.

The bequest describes who gets what. You may bequest certain assets or property to specific people, or you may just say you leave everything to one person. However, if you have personal items—such as a collection of antique rifles your brother-in-law has always admired, a keepsake piece of jewelry you'd like your sister to have, or a refurbished classic car you want to leave to your son—these are all bequests you should state in your will.

Bequests should be specific in naming both the property and the recipient. Also note that while you may own an item at the time you write the will—such as a boat or car—if you sell or trade the item before you pass on, the beneficiary has no claim to it once you've died. Furthermore, if you trade in the Chevy Impala you've bequeathed to your brother for a Pontiac Grand Am, your brother will not automatically inherit the Grand Am unless you update your will and specifically state this.

You may also forgive debts in your will should someone owe you money. If one of your beneficiaries owes you money, your will should clearly state whether that debt is forgiven in full or if the money owed should be subtracted from the amount bequeathed to that individual.

Disinheritance provisions need to be very specific as well. You should clearly name the person and state that he or she will receive nothing. When it comes to disinheriting one or more family members, it's actually a good idea to leave them some small bequest so that they are at least acknowledged in the will. This will help avoid grounds for contesting the will later on with the claim that you simply forgot to include them.

Finally, the "residuary" bequest is when you basically wrap up the rest of your assets and leave them to someone. The language for this type of bequest reads something like, "I leave all the rest of my property to my sister, Julie Smith." This all-inclusive clause ensures that nothing slips through the cracks.

WILL ADMINISTRATION

Wills are like income tax filings—you can pay a little or a lot to have someone help you draft a will, or you can do it completely on your own. Will kits are typically available online or at your garden variety office supply store for a nominal price, and they include a full set of instructions to help you complete the forms.

Wills need to be signed and witnessed by two disinterested parties (three is better), preferably in the presence of a notary. A disinterested party is basically someone who is not named as one of the three entities within the will. The witnesses do not all need to be present at the same time, although it is best if they watch you sign your name to the will and then each sign theirs. A witness does not need to read the will or be there as you draft it. Their main function is to witness that you are sane at the time and claim the will as your own.

It's also a good idea to sign every page of your will to ensure no one can swap out or tamper with pages. Once completed, make several copies of the will and be sure your family members know where you keep the signed original. Plenty of estates have gone into probate because the family members simply didn't know a will was written or where it was stored.

WHEN TO CHANGE YOUR WILL

Changes happen. You fall in love, you fall out of love. Your parents die. Your brother moves to another country. All of these events can affect what's in your will.

You have to remember to keep it up to date. If not, your offspring may wind up as child missionaries in Uganda with your born-again brother and his New Age hippie wife, instead of safely tucked away with your aging but lucid parents down the street and in the same school district.

The following are situations that may trigger the need to update your will:

- You get married. If you live in a state where your spouse gets half of everything, you'll need to update your will if you want to specifically bequest your assets and possessions to your children and other family members and friends.
- You remain unmarried but have a new partner. If your will isn't updated, your partner will not (with few exceptions) inherit anything—including guardianship of your children if you so desire. Without a will or alternate estate plan, your partner will inherit nothing.
- If you're not legally divorced, you'll need to create or update a will once you are.
- If you have another baby, be sure to update or confirm the person named in your will as the personal guardian for the new little one. Consider

whether all your children should have the same guardian, and be sure and state these specifics in your will.

- If you are widowed with stepchildren, bear in mind that unless you legally adopt stepchildren, they have no inheritance rights. You need to specifically name them and your bequests in your will.

- If you sell property that you previously bequeathed in your will, you need to update this fact in your will. By the same token, if you acquire new property, you should detail your specific bequest for this new asset or property in your will. This is especially true of any inheritance or financial windfall you may receive since the last time you updated your will.

- If you change your mind about to whom you want to bequest something, be sure to update your will.

There are two ways to change your will. You can add a "codicil," which is basically a legal addition without changing the original will. The codicil can be used to update your wishes. Codicils can be confusing though, and you must carefully include language that negates any previous wishes, as well as sign and date every new codicil.

The easiest way to update a will is to write a new one with a new date. It's best to destroy your old ones to avoid confusion.

Consider writing your will now as a gift of convenience and compassion for your family in the future. When the worst happens, grief over your death will be tough enough—you don't want your loved ones to suffer the stress of uncertainty resulting from probate. Worse yet, you don't want grandpa asking your children if they know where Mommy kept her will.

Other Documents That Name Beneficiaries

Review all other investments or insurance policies you may own that name a beneficiary, such as life insurance policies, 401(k) plans, IRAs, mutual funds, stock portfolios, annuities, and bank accounts. You can eliminate a lot of time, trouble, and expense for the executor of your estate if your named beneficiary or custodian on each of these accounts matches up with the bequest wishes in your will.

Typically, named beneficiaries on your policies and accounts will supersede your will, even if your will is more up to date. Considering that accounts are opened at different times throughout your lifetime, it is very likely your named beneficiaries may no longer reflect your current wishes, so make a proactive effort to review these accounts and policies and make appropriate changes.

This exercise can also help you inventory all of your assets for the sake of your will and your financial management capabilities, so it is certainly a worthwhile exercise.

LIVING WILL/POWER OF ATTORNEY

Given that you're single, it's all the more important that you prepare a Living Will and appoint someone else to execute "Power of Attorney." Normally, matters such as whether you should remain on life support or be resuscitated in a terminal situation would fall to a spouse. In your situation, it's important to appoint someone you trust to make this decision on your behalf.

A Living Will states whether or not you wish to be sustained by a life support system should you be diagnosed as terminally ill and become too incapacitated to make this decision for yourself.

Durable power of attorney simply assigns someone else of your choosing to make decisions on your behalf when you may no longer do so. These may be financial, medical, or any other type of decision that you would make if you were capable of doing so and could communicate them. Power of attorney decisions as they relate to medical treatment are called a health care proxy.

Again, the last thing you want is for your teenager to be faced with these heart-wrenching decisions in the wake of an already tragic situation. Establishing a living will and power of attorney takes that decision out of the hands of your children.

Bequeath Values as Part of Your Legacy

Succession is about more than just bequeathing your money and your worldly goods. It's also about who will succeed you. Barring major calamity, that would be your children. Therefore, succession is about your legacy, your values, and the imprint you leave on them. Not just what you knowingly teach your children but also what you learned, how you learned it (some good, some bad circumstances), and how you responded, assimilated, and passed on your learnings to your children—both consciously and unconsciously.

For example, my son had a fifth-grade assignment to write on the topic of, "What Makes You Rich?" I didn't know about this assignment until the last day of the school year when he came home with his backpack stuffed with papers. Apparently his teacher had posted his and other student

essays on the wall in the classroom, so this was the first I knew about it.
I couldn't have been prouder (or more surprised!):

March 17, 1999

"What Makes You Rich?"

Having friends and relatives make me rich in different ways. Having a
home and wearing clothes make me rich. Having money is really not
the best way to judge somebody or yourself if you are rich or not.
The food I eat and the things I do make me rich.

—by Wheatley Stefan, fifth grade

TWELVE

Taxes

Not to belittle all the wonderful advantages to being a single parent, but financially speaking, the head of household tax filing may well be the greatest advantage of all.

As single parents normally move about a half step (or more) behind married couples with children, this tax status can put you just a smidgen more ahead. Hey, we take what we can get for the privilege of parenting alone.

In the case of the single parent, you may file as head of household if you are unmarried (or legally separated) by the end of the year and you paid more than half the cost of maintaining the home in which you and your dependent child lived in for at least more than half the year.

Head of household is the most advantageous tax filing status because

- You receive a higher standard deduction—higher than that available to single filers. Married filers receive a higher deduction, but if you divide the deduction by the two filers, it comes out to less than that the head of household receives.
- You receive lower tax rates—each tax bracket has different income ranges based on filer status. In other words, the income range for the 25 percent tax bracket is higher for head of household than it is for singles. Again, married folks receive higher ranges, but it's not proportionate when divided by the two filers.

There are other advantages, such as lower income ranges for certain tax deductions and credits, such as 401(k) and IRA contributions and the

Retirement Savings Contribution Credit ("Saver's Credit"). With the saver's credit, you may receive a tax credit for anywhere from 10 to 50 percent of annual retirement account contributions of up to $2,000 (indexed each year).

Credits are even better than tax deductions. A tax deduction will reduce the amount of income on which you are required to pay taxes, but a credit is a dollar-for-dollar reduction of the money you owe in taxes. If your credits are higher than the taxes owed, you'll receive the balance in the form of a refund (with the exception of some nonrefundable credits, which are not paid out once your tax bill hits zero).

Credits that single parents often qualify for (subject to income limitations and phaseouts) include

- Earned income credit—if you work at least part of the year but don't earn a lot of money;
- Child tax credit—for each child under age 17 at the end of the year;
- Child and dependent care credit—if you paid someone to care for your child so you could work or look for work;
- Adoption credit—for qualifying expenses paid to adopt an eligible child (must exclude employer-reimbursed expenses).

CREDITS AND DEDUCTIONS FOR COLLEGE EXPENSES

Credits

There are two tax credits available for education expenses: The Hope Scholarship and Lifetime Learning Credits.

The Hope Scholarship allows you to claim a tax credit of up to $1,800 (2009) for each eligible dependent for the first two tax years of college attendance—100 percent of the first $1,200 of eligible expenses and 50 percent of the next $1,200. It is a nonrefundable credit—meaning that if it reduces your tax liability below zero, you won't get any balance credit refunded to you.

The Lifetime Learning Credit covers the last two years of college as well as continuing college education for adults taking classes on a full-time or part-time basis to improve or upgrade their job skills. There is no limit to the number of years for which you can claim a lifetime learning credit. This credit allows you to claim up to $2,000 per year for the taxpayer, taxpayer's spouse, or any eligible dependents. A family may claim up to 20 percent of $10,000 of eligible expenses.

You cannot claim both the Hope and Lifetime Learning Credits for the same student in the same year. Plus, bear in mind that for both credits, there are income limits and phaseouts for eligibility and any grant aid is subtracted before the credit is applied. In short, if you qualify for significant grant aid, this may negate your ability to take a credit.

Deductions

You may take the Tuition and Fees Deduction on money borrowed to pay for qualified college expenses, such as a student loan and/or money you pay out of pocket, up to $4,000. In the case of student loans, you may take the credit in the years the expenses are paid, not the years the loan is repaid. There are income limitations and phaseouts indexed annually.

This is great. It means that in addition to borrowing money to pay for college (so you are not forking out the money yourself), you can reduce the income taxes you owe on your current income in those years.

You may also utilize the Student Loan Interest Deduction for the interest on a student loan you used to pay for college expenses if you are the one legally obligated to pay it back. In other words, student loans obligate the student to pay back the loan (even if you actually end up paying it), so only the student can take the interest deduction.

However, your child can take the deduction only if you no longer claim him or her as an exemption on your tax return. Also note that there are income limitations and phaseouts to claim this deduction.

TAXES ON INVESTMENTS

When you sell shares from an investment, be it a stock, mutual fund, or something else, you will most likely incur either a gain or a loss. If your selling price is less than what you originally paid, you incur a loss. Losses may be used as a deduction against gains when filing your tax return.

Capital gains, on the other hand, occur when you sell shares for more than you originally paid. Gains are subject to capital gains taxes.

- Investments held one year or less are considered short-term; capital gains are taxed at your ordinary income rate.
- Investments held over one year are considered long-term; capital gains are taxed at 15 percent (scheduled to increase to 20% in 2010).

The yield or dividend is a share of a company's profits that a stock, bond, or mutual fund pays out to shareholders. Currently (subject to change by 2010), investors in income tax brackets of 25 percent or higher pay a 15 percent tax on dividends. Investors who fall in a lower tax bracket are taxed at a 5 percent rate on dividends.

You may have the option to automatically reinvest dividend payouts directly back into a mutual fund. With a stock portfolio, you may have the option to enroll in a Dividend Reinvestment Plan, or "DRIP," which allows you to use your dividends to automatically buy fractional shares of the same stock.

Some mutual funds offer a cross-reinvestment plan that allows you to use dividends and/or capital gains distributions to reinvest in a different mutual fund(s) within the same fund family. These distributions are considered taxable even though you never actually receive the cash.

You will receive statements from your mutual fund company or brokerage at the end of the year detailing your taxable investments.

Can You Really Learn to File Your Own Tax Return?

A word about taxes: "Yuck." If you think learning about deductions and credits is just completely beyond you, I challenge you to be any more ill-equipped than me. My problems started back in fifth grade when my school, in its infinite wisdom, embarked upon the "open classroom" teaching environment. This is when they tore down the walls and expected students to roam among various "centers" and teach themselves the curriculum for each subject. Teachers were available to help clarify and answer any questions. Hah! Exactly.

For me, the worst of it was arithmetic, where the line to get assistance in teaching yourself math extended clear across the (formerly) three-classroom-length building. Being a natural born word-person, nothing was more foreign or less interesting to me than fractions, decimals, integers, surface area, volume, or percentages. To say that I was ill-prepared for algebra in seventh and ninth grades, with geometry stuck in between, is quite the understatement. In fact, amidst the tutors, the tears, and the embarrassment of a new school and way more smarter friends, math represents a pretty dramatic and bleak time in my life. So much so, that I haven't taken a math class since my freshman year in high school; ducking out of the requirement in college by taking logic (math using words; not much better, but at least it was WORDS).

As a professional writer and lifelong lover of words, I find it rather remarkable (as do my parents) that I've spent the last 15 years of my career writing for the financial industry. It just goes to show you that willingness, exposure, and frankly, the realization that failure is not an option can propel you to learn and succeed when you put your mind to it.

In short, if I can learn to do my tax return, so can you.

TAX PREPARATION

One of the most excruciating times of the year is that crunch right before April 15 when Americans scramble to produce accurate and timely tax returns. One of the most important decisions you can make is whether to complete your return yourself or hire the expertise of a tax professional.

With the Internet, it's getting much easier to file returns yourself than it used to be. Not only are there user-friendly software and sites that allow you to file returns electronically, but there are a wealth of educational Web sites where you may learn more about the filing process, the claims and deductions for which you may qualify, and download required forms.

When you use an online tax return service, all you have to do is answer questions. Your answers will automatically trigger more questions and forms to complete for the credits and deductions available to you—you don't have to figure them all out for yourself.

Better yet, online access means no more trips to the library or post office to find they don't stock or are out of the forms you need. Now, everything can be done at home. In fact, the IRS Web site (www.irs.gov) has all the forms and publications you need, and it's written in very user-friendly language with a comprehensive search engine to help you locate specific information.

The best thing about learning to do your taxes yourself is that this is an educational experience you may build upon each year. What may at first seem intimidating becomes more commonplace each year, and you only need to learn any new tax updates and regulations.

And, frankly, the credits and deductions for head of household filers just seem to get better and better, so it's a pleasure to seek out new changes. High-earning, double-income married couples probably don't feel the same way, so enjoy the tax preparation advantages of being a single parent.

Whom Do You Call?

If you itemize expenses, have complex investments, or are self-employed, your tax return may not be quite so simple. In this case, you should gauge how valuable your time is and whether you want to spend it learning all the nuances of tax law that apply to your situation or simply turn the burden over to a seasoned professional.

If you decide to go the professional route, you still have quite a few decisions to make. First of all, don't just go to the phone book and call up the first tax preparer in the yellow pages. Take some time to find out what type of tax pro is best suited for your situation, and ask friends, family, and coworkers for recommendations for a good tax professional. Tax preparers are like dentists: You can have a good or bad experience depending entirely upon whom you choose.

The following is a primer to help you determine which type of tax professional is appropriate for your situation, listed loosely in general terms from the least to the most expensive.

- Tax Preparer—This is your basic H&R Block or Jackson Hewitt franchisee. These preparers may or may not have a college education or professional training in tax law, so it's a bit of a crapshoot as to whether you'll get a really good one or not. However, all of these pros must meet the franchise's requirements, which generally include refresher courses each year in preparation for tax season.

- Accountant—Like tax preparers, not all accountants are created equally. Some have a college education; others do not. Some have tax law training, some just keep the books for small businesses. What's important here is to find one that specializes in personal taxes, and you may indeed find someone just as good as an expensive CPA.

- Financial Advisor—Most of these pros just stick to investment and money management advice, but a few specialize in personal taxes as well. This is particularly beneficial because they will have a clear picture of your total financial well-being, and may integrate your tax and investment picture to your best advantage. However, personal tax experts in this field are few and far between, so shop carefully and check references.

- Enrolled Agent—An enrolled agent is the one you'll want by your side if you tend to be aggressive in your returns. To become an enrolled agent, this pro needs to have worked for the IRS for at least five years or have passed a rigorous exam that's comparable to the bar. Enrolled agents tend to be extremely well qualified and knowledgeable about personal taxes, and are the only tax preparation specialists allowed to represent a taxpayer before the IRS during an audit (CPAs and attorneys are also allowed). You may search for an enrolled agent at the Web site for the National Association of Enrolled Agents (www.naea.org). Most states also have enrolled agent agencies and accompanying Web sites.

- Tax Attorney and/or CPA—At the top of the totem pole are these two types of professionals who must meet specific educational and exam requirements to achieve their designations. While they tend to be more expensive, both tax attorneys and CPAs are generally more knowledge-able and experienced in their areas of expertise. However, here you must be careful as well. Ask plenty of questions before making your choice, because not all tax attorneys and CPAs specialize in personal tax law.

WHAT YOU NEED TO FILE

To be a pack rat, or not to be a pack rat, that is the question. All things even, the IRS would prefer that you save everything relating to your tax returns for all eternity.

That's not entirely true, but close. Most tax advisors will advise you to save your tax returns and related receipts and forms for up to three years after filing. However, there are extenuating circumstances to even this guideline.

Technically, the IRS may audit you for up to six years after a filing if it believes you underreported your income by up to 25 percent or more. But it gets worse. If you do not file a return or file a fraudulent return where you intentionally misreport your income, there is no statute of limitations on when the IRS can audit you.

Keep in mind that this is a your-word-versus-theirs scenario. You may feel confident that your tax returns are accurate, but they may see things differently. And unfortunately, with the IRS, you're guilty until proven otherwise. If your proof is the burden of maintaining tax records, then you pretty much better keep everything . . . pretty much forever.

What to Keep

While you're supposed to keep bank records up to three to seven years anyway, keep in mind that your checkbooks are also a good record of your income and expenses. Online records that you print out aren't always deemed acceptable, and most banks limit the transaction history you can access anyway.

Naturally, you want to keep a copy of your tax returns and any accom-panying forms, receipts, and documentation to verify the accuracy of the return.

This is true even if you file your return using computer software or online resources. You'll want to back up your files onto a separate storage device, and also keep paper copies of the actual forms and receipts used to compile your return.

The following is a list of basic records you should organize by year and have on hand in case you do get audited in the future:

- W-2 Forms
- 1099 Forms
- Bank statements
- Brokerage/mutual fund statements
- Invoices and receipts used for tax preparation
- Past tax returns
- Canceled checks/proof of payment of taxes paid each year
- Interest statements for your mortgage and any home equity loans
- Home sale/purchase and insurance documents
- Casualty and theft loss claims
- Mortgage statements and tax assessments
- Child care receipts
- Records of donations and other noncash charitable contributions
- Bills/receipts for medical and dental expenses, as well as documented transportation costs

HEAD OF HOUSEHOLD TIP: TAX PREP

If your taxes recently took a turn to the more complicated, consider farming out the preparation of your return this year and using it as a base to learn to do it for yourself next year.

THIRTEEN

Conclusion

A growing number of single people are choosing to head a family-filled household. Despite being single, there are the distinct advantages of raising your children the way you want without the considerations or interference of another adult, spending your own money however you wish, and taking whatever vacations you desire without compromise—just to mention a few.

All nice perks indeed. The fact is that single parent living can be as challenging and rewarding and enjoyable as any other lifestyle, including marriage. I understand that some folks like that, too.

I also understand that some folks gave marriage a whirl but have found that single parenting is a better alternative for the lifestyle and independence they seek.

But the demands and challenges of being head of the household are also numerous. With all the day-to-day responsibilities of carpools and grocery shopping and just plain earning a living, it can be tough finding the time and energy to look down the road, plan for the long term, and make those tough decisions. But it is necessary.

One of the important things to remember is that money isn't the key to happiness. Lots of people with lots of money are not happy at all. Most people are just looking for someone to love. As a parent, you already have that. That makes you richer than so many others who want what you have.

"LOVE-YA-BYE"

There comes a time when most children no longer want you to kiss them, or hug them, or tell them you love them—especially not in front of their friends. With my eldest son, this happened around age 10. So I compromised; I would say it really, really fast whenever I was leaving him. It came out: "Love-ya-bye." He found this acceptable and adopted it as well.

One day around age 12 he was talking with a friend on the phone, and when they hung up, my son accidentally said, "Love-ya-bye." His friend called him right back, laughing hysterically, and asked him if he had just said what he thought he had just said.

This turned into a catchphrase between the two boys, one they playfully chanted anytime they were at school, football practice, chatting up girls— whatever and wherever. It became a "thing."

Thankfully, it is still a "thing" to this day. Even away at college, my son still has no problem talking to me on his cell phone and saying "Love-ya-bye" while standing amidst a room full of fraternity brothers.

I wouldn't trade this for $10 million.

Don't ever take the privilege of parenthood for granted. The money, well that's just something you manage. And just like parenting, you build on your experience of making financial mistakes and get better at it every year.

Consider your financial education, much like your parent learning curve, a lifelong process. And, you have to take this education very seriously. You wouldn't stop parenting for a day, or a week, or a month. So don't lose your focus when it comes to disciplined saving and spending wisely.

Keep researching and learning about money management, investment options, and the joy of earning passive income so that you can actively spend more time with your children. Learn the value of staying on top of your finances—not always behind the eight ball—and you will inherently pass this value on to your children.

Consider the top three values a single parent can pass on to his or her children:

1. Eating well
2. Regular exercise
3. Money management

None of these values cost money to achieve. You don't have to be well educated or earn a high income to master them and pass them on to your children. You just have to stay focused, disciplined, and prioritize these values in your life.

Honestly, I think one- to two-year courses in each of these subjects should be mandatory in both high school and college.

Napoleon Schmapolean; Latin Schmatin.

Let's teach our children something that they'll remember and find useful in their everyday lives for as long as they live.

Maybe everyone won't prioritize these values, but single parents can. Make it your mark in the world; your contribution to the evolution of single parents. Your legacy as a single parent can yield a new generation of children who care about what they eat, care about how they spend their time, and care about how they spend their money.

Pretty soon, children of single parents can make *their* mark in the world—all because the single parent isn't distracted by fancy cars or big houses or large-screen TVs. You can enhance the way single parents are perceived by improving your own life, your values, and thus the values your children hold dear and pass on to their children. This is how we, as single parents, can make a difference.

You may not have realized it yet, but as a single parent you live a charmed life. You get the joy of raising a family and all the liberating independence that comes with making your own choices and decisions about who to spend your time with as an adult, how to spend your money, and how to raise your children. It's the best of both the single world and the married world, and it's yours to enjoy if you adapt the right mind-set.

Like I said, it's about values. Value your life as a single parent.

APPENDIX

Resources

Federal Citizen Information Center: www.pueblo.gsa.gov
> Tons of accurate information about all kinds of stuff, the Federal Citizen Information Center (FCIC) brings together an array of U.S. government information and services and makes them accessible to the public via Internet, e-mail, mail, or phone.

BUDGET

Budgeting Software: http://Quicken.Intuit.com
Budgeting worksheets: http://www.betterbudgeting.com/budgetforms free-basicbudgeting.htm
> http://office.microsoft.com (search "budget" for free templates you can download)

CHILD CARE

The National Association of Child Care Resource and Referral Agencies: http://naccrra.org
YMCA: http://ymca.net
> You can search for a local YMCA via this site.
Jewish Community Centers: http://www.jcca.org
> You can search for a JCC near you via this site.
Local Parent Magazine: http://localparentmagazine.com
Dependent care flexible spending account, IRS Publication 503, *Child and Dependent Care Expenses*: http://www.irs.gov/publications/p503

CREDIT

Federal Trade Commission: www.ftc.gov/credit

List of approved debt counselors: www.usdoj.gov/ust/eo/bapcpa/ccde/
de_approved.htm

Debt reduction worksheet: www.adshq.org/content/monthly_worksheet.pdf

Bankrate.com credit card calculators: www.bankrate.com/brm/rate/
cc_home.asp

Annual Credit Report: http://www.annualcreditreport.com
Order free copies of all three credit reports each year.

HEALTH

IRS Publication 969, *Health Savings Accounts and Other Tax-Favored
Health Plans*: www.irs.gov/pub/irs-pdf/p969.pdf

COBRA, U.S. Department of Labor: www.dol.gov/dol/topic/health-plans/
cobra.htm

HOUSING

National Association of Realtors: www.realtor.com
Good search site for nationwide MLS real estate listings.

For Sale By Owner: www.fsbo.com
Popular site for properties being sold by homeowners without real
estate agents.

Homefair: www.homefair.com
An online resource for all things related to home buying, renting,
moving, and comparing schools.

Domania: www.domania.com
Provides free home prices, house value tools, mortgage tools, MLS
listings, and other real estate services. Can help you conduct your
own CMA.

Zillow: www.zillow.com
Search homes for sale, home prices, home values, recently sold homes,
mortgage rates, and more. Can help you conduct your own CMA.

American Society of Home Inspectors: www.ashi.com
Search for a local home inspector.

Lendingtree.com: www.lendingtree.com
Connects borrowers with multiple loan offers in order to compare
options.

Eloan.com: www.eloan.com

Connects borrowers with multiple loan offers in order to compare options.

A. M. Best: www.ambest.com

Provides online access to bank ratings, data, special reports, and news on the banking industry.

Federal Reserve Bank of San Francisco: www.frbsf.org/publications/consumer/pmi.html

For information about new regulations relating to private mortgage insurance.

IRS Publication 936, *Home Mortgage Interest Deduction*: http://www.irs.gov/pub/irs-pdf/p936.pdf

INCOME

IRS Publication 587, *Business Use of Your Home*: www.irs.gov/publications/p587

Small Business Administration: www.sba.gov

Foreclosures: U.S. Department of Housing and Urban Development: www.hud.gov/homes/homesforsale.cfm

INSURANCE

Fair Access to Insurance Requirement: www.iii.org

Kelley Blue Book: www.kbb.com

Edmunds.com: www.edmunds.com

Automotive information Web site that publishes new and used automotive pricing guides, including vehicle reviews.

Insure.com: www.insure.com

Allows you to compare quotes for various types of insurance policies from multiple issuers all at one site.

NetQuote: www.netquote.com

Allows you to compare quotes for various types of insurance policies from multiple issuers all at one site.

INVESTING

Vanguard Family of Funds: www.vanguard.com

Free Application for Federal Student Aid: www.fafsa.ed.gov

College Savings Plans Network: www.collegesavings.org

An online source of information for state-operated college savings programs.

Upromise: www.upromise.com
> Open an account and accumulate savings for college from eligible purchases you make every day.

Yahoo! Finance: www.finance.yahoo.com
> Comprehensive site to keep up with daily investment news and track your portfolio.

Social Security Administration: http://ssa.gov

Financial Planning Association: http://www.fpanet.org/Membership/Planner Search
> Online referral service is designed to help consumers find Certified Financial Planner professionals.

National Association of Personal Financial Advisors: http://findan advisor.napfa.org
> Search for fee-based financial planning professionals.

American Society of CLU and ChFC: http://www.financialpro.org/ Consumer/find.cfm
> Consumer referral service provides names and contact information of credentialed advisors by ZIP code.

Certified Financial Planner Board of Standards: www.cfp.net/search
> Find individuals currently authorized by CFP Board to use the Certified Financial Planner certification marks. Planners who have been publicly disciplined by the CFP Board will also be listed with an indicator of disciplinary action.

FINRA: www.finra.org/brokercheck
> Check out the background of an investment professional.

SAVING

Autobytel: www.autobytel.com
> Research new and used cars.

AutoTrader: www.autotrader.com
> Research new and used cars.

CarMax: www.carmax.com
> Research new and used cars.

SUCCESSION

Holographic wills—state approvals: www.lawchek.com/Library1/_books/ probate/qanda/holographic.htm

TAXES

IRS: www.irs.gov

National Association of Enrolled Agents: www.naea.org

> Search for an Enrolled Agent with technical expertise in the field of taxation and approved by the U.S. Department of the Treasury to represent taxpayers before all administrative levels of the Internal Revenue Service for audits, collections, and appeals.

Index

About the Author

Kara Stefan is a freelance writer specializing in the financial services and insurance industries. She holds a BA in English from the College of Charleston and has led an extensive career as a marketing communications professional. She is a single mother of two boys and lives in Virginia.

INDEPENDENCE TOWNSHIP LIBRARY
6495 CLARKSTON ROAD
CLARKSTON, MI 48346-1501